Whistleblower: Justice over Discrimination and Ethics Violations

DENNIS PATTERSON

ISBN: 1500111279
ISBN-13: 978-1500111274

DEDICATION

To my beautiful wife. I will be forever grateful for your unconditional love, encouragement and support. Together we shared the pain of the hardships and the joy of the victories. Our love not only endured it grew stronger.

The man of integrity walks securely, but he who takes crooked paths will be found out.

Proverbs 10: 9 (NIV)

"The ultimate measure of a man is not where he stands in times of comfort and convenience, but where he stands in times of challenge and controversy."

Dr. Martin Luther King Jr.

"Injustice anywhere is a threat to justice everywhere."

Dr. Martin Luther King Jr.

PROLOGUE

Sometime during the second half of 2004, the U.S.
Department of Energy (DOE) reached an agreement with
Battelle Energy Alliance (BEA) to take over the
management of the Idaho National Engineering and
Environmental Laboratory (INEEL). On February 1,
2005, the facility was officially renamed the Idaho National
Laboratory (INL) and BEA took over operations from
Bechtel. The following day Idaho Governor, Dirk
Kempthorne, U. S. Senator Larry Craig, and Congressman
Mike Simpson signed a letter declaring February 2, 2005,
"Idaho National Laboratory Day."

It was a memorable day for Idaho Falls. But to the
8,000 INL employees, it was memorable for a very
different reason. Included in the announcements – BEA
had been selected to transform the INL into the nation's
pre-eminent Nuclear Research, development, and
demonstration laboratory.

The message was clear; BEA management would
transform the INL. Some jobs would be realigned, some
jobs eliminated. It was a time of turmoil throughout the
geographically largest DOE facility – 569,135 acres of high
mountain desert that enveloped a portion of four Idaho
counties west of Idaho Falls. Contributing to the turmoil
was the fact that the laboratory had been split into two
major components. The first was the INL, focused on
research and development. The second, the Idaho
Cleanup Project (ICP) focused on environmental cleanup.

I was more excited about the new opportunities than
concerned about my job. I was a long time employee of

the facility and for the past 10 years, Manager of Ethics and Employee Concerns. This was also an exciting time in my personal life. Seven months earlier, after being a divorced dad for several years, I had married the love of my life, LaVonna. My daughter Jasmine was eleven years old and my son Darius was thirteen. Both were healthy and happy. Our future seemed bright.

Over the years, I had been recognized for my commitment to excellence and outstanding work performance. My contributions had made a difference in the lives of our employees and in the overall work environment at the Laboratory. I reported to one of the BEA directors who were part of the transition team. He had assured me early on, that my job was secure and I would continue reporting to him.

I was proud of my job and proud to be a part of the INL. The Idaho laboratory had a proud history. It was established in 1949 as the National Reactor Testing Station. Two short years later, it created the world's first usable electricity from nuclear energy. Since then, it has become one of 10 multi-program national laboratories owned by the U.S. Department of Energy (DOE). It had become a premier, science-based, applied engineering national laboratory dedicated to supporting the U.S. Department of Energy's missions in energy research, nuclear science and national defense.

Excluding State government, we were the largest employer in Idaho. About 25% of Eastern Idaho's employment was connected to the laboratory. Annually, our employees contributed, nearly $2 billion of personal income to the region. Our people were generally better educated, better paid, and willingly became involved in local issues. The INL was recognized as a vital stabilizing economic force throughout Eastern Idaho.

INL's vision to become a world-class nuclear laboratory by 2015 would ensure continued growth. A stated guiding principle to "respect and care for our people," would promote integrity in a work force that would radiate into surrounding communities. I was getting the opportunity to lead the Ethics and Employee Concerns program for a company that was going to lead the laboratory to a grand and glorious new day.

The ink was hardly dry on the contract, when I investigated, identified and reported violations of federal regulations and laboratory policy. Because the violations were so egregious, I wanted to meet with the INL President/Laboratory Director. When I told this to a BEA senior manager, he was opposed to the meeting.

"Do you really want to take me on," he said.

After taking a deep breath, I responded, "What do you mean?

"I will challenge your credibility" he said.

"I will stand on my credibility and integrity," I replied.

Rather than correct the mistakes, and recognize me for doing my job, BEA senior management chose to intimidate and then retaliate.

With my back to the wall, I resorted to an action that at no time in my long career at the site, did I think possible. I became a whistleblower. This is my story of a long and painful fight for justice, fairness and for a better INL, and along the way for a better community. It is also a story about the wonderful experiences and people that were part of the journey, a journey that I couldn't have survived without my faith, family and friends.

Chapter 1 - Injustice

It was the afternoon of Thursday, February 24, 2005. I was sitting at my desk. It had been a slow day. In fact, there hadn't been any ethics issues reported since BEA took over the contract. It was near the end of the day and I was thinking about what LaVonna might prepare for dinner and what the kids might want me to do that evening. The loud ring of the "ethics hotline" startled me. "Dennis Patterson, Ethics and Employee Concerns," I answered, fully expecting it to be a routine matter that I could take care of in just a matter of minutes. Little did I realize that this call would have a dramatic impact on my professional and personal life and on the future of the Laboratory.

"I need someone to help me."

The voice was a mix of anger, confusion, and desperation. He said he was a construction worker and his name was Loren. He had just been terminated from his job at the Laboratory; his access badge pulled, and was physically escorted from the premises.

"I need help," Loren blurted. "No one will tell me why I've been removed from the site." When he asked the supervisor who escorted him from the premises, the terse response was ... "You know why." Loren explained that on his way home he called BEA Personnel Security supervisor, Jodi. She told him, "It's because of your felony and ongoing problems with the law." Loren explained to

her that he had been similarly escorted from the
Laboratory work site eight years ago (1997) due to a 1994
felony conviction. He assured her that his access had been
restored in 1998 when he was no longer on probation.
According to Loren, none of this information seemed to
matter to Jodi. She refused to provide him any further
information, even though Personnel Security had
seasonally issued him an INL access badge every year since
1998. He received his most recent badge approximately a
month prior to this call.

In his efforts to get an answer, Loren contacted
the lead attorney for the Idaho Cleanup Project (ICP),
Dennis Love. He was told, "We don't have to tell you
anything ... Idaho is a right to work state." Loren said he
was also told there was no appeal process.

"Dennis, can you find out why I was removed and
if there is any way to appeal?" Loren asked. I assured
Loren that the matter would be thoroughly reviewed and
answers provided.

I knew that I needed to inform my boss, Doug
Benson, director of Internal Audits. I deemed this
necessary for a couple of reasons. First, the issue involved
the actions of BEA Personnel Security and the acting
General Counsel of ICP. Second, Loren was a distant
relative of mine and hence someone might think I couldn't
be objective and impartial.

From personal experience, I was also concerned
that some of my colleagues might see this as one African
American trying to help another. Such biased thinking had
caused problems in the past.

Benson and I decided to consult with BEA

General Counsel, Mark Olsen. Benson placed a speaker phone call to Olsen and we reviewed the facts. It was agreed that it would be appropriate for me to find out why Loren was escorted from the site, and if there was an appeal process.

We also discussed my family relationship with Loren. I told them that his mother was a cousin of mine, but Loren and I barely knew each other. We expected that this would be a simple procedure review and then someone would inform Loren why his access was revoked. My past experience with such matters led me to believe this issue would be resolved in a few hours or at most a couple of days.

When I returned to my office, I decided the first step would be to contact Jodi. I was confident she would share the reason(s) for revoking Loren's access and that due process had been followed consistent with BEA security procedures. The next morning I invited her to my office. Jodi and I had known each other for many years. Thus, I began by sharing some life pleasantries and asked how she was doing. The conversation was relaxed and comfortable – until I asked her about Loren.

She explained that the primary reason for revoking his site access was his 1994 felony. She said that Loren had "ongoing problems with the law" such as trespassing and burglary. This answer bewildered me because Loren had explained to me he was taken off probation in 1998 and had been working seasonably at the lab every year since without any problems. It made no sense that he would lie about something that could easily be checked out. I asked Jodi whether these "problems with the law" were recent. With a quizzical look on her face, she replied, "I don't know."

She reiterated that Loren had a "pattern of

problems with the law." "Scum bags shouldn't be working
here" she added. Did she think Loren was a scumbag?
"What kind of people do you want working at the Lab?"
Jodi said. "Those who meet the criteria defined in our
procedures," I responded.

Jodi confirmed that Personnel Security had issued
Loren an access badge every year since 1998. She
emphasized that the decision to revoke the access was not
just her own. She stated authoritatively that she consulted
with and received concurrence from ICP attorney, Julie
Piper. At the end of the meeting I asked if I could review
Loren's personnel security file so that I could validate and
verify his supposed ongoing problems with the law. I
received an abrupt and terse, "no."

Later that same day, Loren called and asked if he
could stop by and show me his county court records. We
met in a room near Jodi's office. The documents revealed
that he had a felony conviction in 1994 for working while
receiving unemployment benefits and that he had been off
probation since 1998. There were several misdemeanor
violations during 1992 through 1994, including trespassing
and battery. However, what caught my attention was that
since 1998 the only offenses were fishing with two poles,
running a stop sign, and a speeding ticket.

"Looks like you've turned your life around over
the past few years." I commented.

"Yea, I decided it was time to grow up and be a
good example and father for my kids. Now, I just want to
go back to work."

The next day I invited Jodi back to my office to
explain what appeared to be a number of unanswered

questions. I handed her Loren's court records. After reviewing them, she declared that she still believed that he had a pattern of problems with the law. I agreed that from 1992 to 1994 he definitely had a string of legal problems. I asked if I could see Loren's file.

"No." she barked.

I asked, "Is there an appeal process for construction workers?"

Defiantly, she said, "No, there is not."

I ended the interview. Later that afternoon, I briefed Benson on the tone and content of my discussion with Jodi. He seemed surprised by what I told him, but didn't express any particular concern.

A couple of days later, Loren's local union representative called me.

"Dennis Patterson, Employee Concerns," I answered.

"Hey, are you Pat's son?" Pat is the name my father was known by throughout the city. My dad had been a member of this same laborer's union for fifty years.

"Yes," I proudly responded. The caller told me how well liked and respected my dad was. After a brief stroll down memory lane we discussed Loren's situation. He explained that BEA did have an appeal procedure and that it had been used in the past for resolving similar problems. He stated his belief that Loren wasn't being treated fairly. He said there were other union workers, on the same job as Loren, with a lot worse criminal histories. He said he would fax me a copy of the BEA procedure.

After hanging up, I leaned back in my chair and

closed my eyes.   It had been awhile since I had thought
about my dad. He had passed on April 21, 2003, in the
Veterans home in Pocatello.

My dad was a rough and tough man that took no
guff from anyone. He wasn't one to show much emotion,
but he loved his family. He was known throughout the
community for his hard work, honesty and integrity. My
eyes misted as I remembered the final months of his life.
Dad had developed dementia in his last years and we had
to place him in the Veterans home. As his mental abilities
slipped, he wasn't able to communicate very much. But
the one thing he could say right up until the end was
"Buzzy." That was the name he had called me since I was
a little boy. If only I could hear him say "Buzzy" one
more time.

Of course thoughts of dad brought back thoughts
of my mom. She had died eleven months before dad.
Mom was loving, caring, compassionate, and giving. No
matter what the circumstance or situation she was always
there for her family.   All of us five kids were with her
when she passed on May 26, 2002. On her last day she
had me lean down to her bed, "Promise me you will keep
the family together," she whispered.   "I promise, I love
you mom," I responded.

Family had always been the most important thing
for Mom. Her mother had died when she was young and
so she helped raise her siblings. Both her parents were
members of the Rosebud Sioux Indian Nation.   When
Mom and Dad wanted to get married they couldn't
because he was Black and there were laws against
interracial marriage where they lived. They had to go to a
different state in order to legally marry and begin their life

together. This was part of my family heritage.

Later that afternoon I received the fax from the union representative, "BEA Appeal Process for Construction Workers." Upon reviewing the procedure, it was clear to me that it was applicable to Loren's case. If followed properly, the appeal process would help resolve Loren's problem.

I then met with Jodi's boss, Lynn Goldman and suggested that he convene an appeal hearing per the guidance in the procedure. Goldman dismissively told me, "this procedure doesn't apply to Loren." Annoyed and exasperated, I challenged his opinion, "Of course it applies. He's a construction worker!" Goldman continued to disagree and walked off with a shrug of indifference.

Several days later sanity prevailed and an appeal hearing was convened. I was invited to attend along with Jodi, Dennis Love, Julie Piper (ICP attorney), BEA Human Resources director, ICP Human Resources director, Benson and a couple of others. I had reservations about this meeting but I believed that justice would prevail. The evidence was clear: Loren had been granted access for the past eight years and had only very minor problems with the law during that time. Not only that, the relevant company procedure was clear in stating that a person with a felony could work at the laboratory as long as they were no longer on probation. Equally compelling, Loren's work history was void of any performance or behavior problems.

I entered the meeting confident that there would be a fair and just outcome. I came prepared with Loren's arrest record, relevant procedures and a copy of the INL Standards of Conduct and Business Ethics (SOCBE). I expected to attend the entire meeting. However, after I provided the information, I was told, "Dennis you can

leave now." But before leaving, I quoted from the
SOCBE, reminding everyone of their own, and the
company's, obligation to demonstrate the highest level of
honesty and integrity. I went back to my office expecting
to hear good news within the next couple of hours.

After waiting most of the day I contacted the
Labor Relations representative, who said, "The appeal was
denied." I fell back in my chair and almost tipped over. I
couldn't believe what I heard.

"Why was it denied?" I asked

He paused, "after you left the meeting someone
said Loren had five problems with the law that he didn't
report on his security paperwork."

"What are the problems and when did they
occur."

He replied, "We were instructed not to tell
anyone, but the information is public record."

I left work and went down to the Bonneville
county courthouse and reviewed Loren's public records.
Upon entering the building I went upstairs to the law
library and logged onto the computer. As I looked at the
computer screen, it was clear that what I saw was an exact
match of the documents Loren had provided. I was
outraged at the outcome of appeal hearing and the
apparent miscarriage of justice.

Upon returning to work, I went to Benson's office
and shared the results of the appeal hearing and my
research. I didn't know that he already knew the results of
the hearing. Over the next several minutes our voices

raised and our passion rose to the surface. Benson's face turned red and his eyes glared. He was relentless in his defense of the decision and the decision makers. I was equally relentless in my position that we needed to investigate further.

"We've done all we are required to do, we followed procedure and held the appeal hearing," Benson declared.

"Doug, it's not about some damn procedure, it's about doing the right thing," I returned to my office only long enough to turn off my computer. I left for home disappointed, frustrated, and angry.

That night I tossed and turned, wondering what tomorrow would bring. Would Benson support me on this or would he insist that I let it go? The next morning when I turned on my work computer, I got my answer. I was relieved when I read the email Benson sent to Goldman. He told him the ethics office would not be closing the case until we knew what the alleged problems with the law were.

CHAPTER 2 – Protection and Deception

Based on the facts, this was an egregious miscarriage of justice. The biggest challenge was that it involved senior level managers and senior attorneys for BEA and ICP. It appeared that people were willing to do anything to protect their jobs, reputations, and to avoid having to admit to wrongdoing. One of my first actions was to begin to document my communications with Olsen and Benson. In emails, I expressed my concern that there was the potential for legal liability for BEA. I detailed

problems including violations of BEA procedures, abuse
of authority, failure to cooperate with my investigation,
and possibly discrimination. Possible federal laws violated
included the Privacy Act and the Freedom of Information
Act. I was hopeful that BEA General Counsel, Mark
Olsen would quickly intervene and reduce the risk to the
company. Boy was I ever wrong!

During the next few weeks I tried to get someone,
anyone, to see that Loren had been the victim of a
grievous injustice. Unfortunately, the response was quite
the opposite. I now, was targeted as the "wrong doer."

Benson informed me that my colleagues were
claiming that I was wrong for being involved with this
matter because Loren was a relative. I reminded him that I
had disclosed my family relationship from the very
beginning. I referred to the BEA Employee Handbook
wherein the definition of immediate family did not include
children of cousins. Finally, I mentioned my concern that
perhaps it was others that weren't being objective and
impartial.

I pointed out Olsen's close relationship with
Dennis Love. Prior to BEA assuming the Laboratory
contract, Love and Piper worked for Olsen for several
years. Approximately six months before the contract
transition, Olsen left the laboratory and Love was
appointed Acting General Counsel. On February 1, 2005,
Olsen returned to his role as General Counsel and Love
became General Counsel for ICP. My point to Benson
was that perhaps Olsen was reluctant to challenge the
decision of his former subordinates, Piper and Love.

Benson seemed to discount all of my concerns.

The focus was now on me. I was the trouble maker. No one seemed at all concerned about Loren. I wondered if things would be different if Loren was a relative of theirs or was someone of importance rather than a Black construction worker.

A member of BEA's legal staff told me that INL Laboratory Director John Grossenbacher would be more concerned about my family relationship with Loren than anything else. Was this a thinly veiled effort to intimidate me and get me to back off my pursuit of justice for Loren?

In spite of all the resistance, I had to pursue this matter because it was the right thing to do and it was my job. The INL Standards of Conduct and Business Ethics required that I take action. My personal ethical and moral compass would not let me do otherwise. In my mind, there was no other way to go but forward.

This was a very difficult time. LaVonna and I were worried about the potential impact on our family. We spent much time in prayer. In the end, we knew that God would protect us if we stayed true to his Word. We knew that regardless of what happened we would always have our faith, our family and our friends.

A couple of weeks after the appeal hearing, Benson sent this email to me:

> *"Dennis Love indicated there were other factors, he left things out of his application. The implication was the individual falsified his application. That is enough for a site walk-off for me, but I don't recall that ever coming up in discussions with Jodie."*

I told Benson that I thought Love was attempting to defend and protect his friends and colleagues instead of promoting fairness. I informed Benson that my investigation had revealed that Loren's security application was filled out by a Personnel Security staff member. This person had a copy of Loren's court records. As such, Loren couldn't have left out any information even if he wanted to.

Love had sent emails to Benson wherein he refused to disclose the five alleged problems with the law. Further, Love was adamant in his position that Benson and I had no right to see Loren's personnel security file. Perhaps Love was trying to protect his friends because they made a serious mistake when they decided to remove Loren from the INL work site without due process.

The most confounding part of Love's actions was the fact that he had no authority to make decisions about access to BEA records. He was the acting General Counsel for ICP and thus had no responsibility or authority related to BEA security files. Yet, he was acting as a roadblock to the records that could put this matter to rest. Even more surprising was that BEA's General Counsel seemed unwilling to take any action. And Benson, BEA director of Internal Audit, was equally reluctant to act.

I was increasingly frustrated about how things were going. Loren's case could be cleared up at a moment's notice if Benson and/or I were allowed to look at the file. If there were problems with the law that he failed to disclose we could tell him what they were. This would be more than enough reason to deny his access to the INL.

We were now approaching mid April 2005. I would turn 50 on April 14. As the days and weeks passed, I became more and more worried about how this would turn out. The morning of the 14th I received an email from Benson. The email was one he received from Love:

> *"While it is true that I agreed that if they need access information in the file in the performance of their duty, I also clearly stated that I do not believe that they need access to the file in this case because all of the concerns have been addressed. I specifically mentioned that I am aware of cases where the Inspector General wanted access to certain Privacy Act files on individuals as part of their investigation but the court found that they did not need them in performing their duty. Please explain why they need access."*

Benson responded to me at 10:45 a.m.:

> *"Dennis Love considers the issue closed and remains of the opinion that 'nothing' can or should be shared from the file."*

"Damn, what a way to begin my fiftieth birthday" I said aloud, hoping that no one heard me as they passed by my office. I shut down my computer and left for home. I needed to be home with the love and encouragement of my family. I was hoping for a quiet evening at home with LaVonna and the kids.

When LaVonna got home from work she said, "Let's go out to dinner." I didn't really want to go out, but when the kids yelled "yea" I couldn't say no. We ended up at Cavanaugh's restaurant. When we entered the room, friends and family jumped up and yelled "Surprise!" I was definitely surprised. I was also glad that Lavonna had invited everyone to celebrate my birthday with us.

Benson and his wife Cindy were among those in attendance. Benson and I had been friends for the past several years. In spite of the work difficulties, it was good to see him. I had also developed a good relationship with Cindy over the years.

It was a fun evening with lots of laughs and good stories. Those few hours were a great respite from the trials and tribulations I was going through. However, there were moments of pause when I would look at Benson and wondered if he would do the right thing with the Loren issue. Would he have the courage to stand up to Love and the BEA senior managers?

Finally, on April 22, 2005, Benson and I were allowed to have access to Loren's personnel security file. We scrutinized every page, looking for problems with the law that would prohibit Loren from working at the site. As we flipped over the last page we looked at each other. Benson's jaw dropped and his face went white. I sensed that he felt betrayed by his friends and colleagues. Loren had no reportable problem with the law since 1997. In fact, there were notes in the record confirming that Loren had been granted access to the INL shortly after getting off probation in 1998. The file fully supported Loren's statements.

Benson and I went to Jodi's office. As she looked up her face was flushed and her lip seemed to quiver. Benson began, "we completed our review and found nothing to support the contention that Loren had ongoing problems with the law."

She looked away and up at the ceiling. Benson continued, "How do you explain this?"

"Well, he's either been lucky and hasn't been caught or has learned how to manipulate the system," Jodi said.

Cold chills went through my body. Did I really hear what I thought I heard?

The silence in the room was deafening.

As we prepared to leave Jodi said, "Dennis doesn't like me - if he saw me in the parking lot he'd probably like to run me over."

I expected Benson to respond. He didn't. We adjourned to our respective offices.

Later when discussing the interview, I told Benson I believed the comments made by Jodi were unprofessional, inappropriate and discriminatory. I told him the remarks indicated a racial bias. Regarding the comment towards me, I told him I felt I was being seen as the stereotypical "angry black man."

Benson gave me a blank stare, then changed the topic to the content of Loren's file. He said he would

inform Goldman of the results. He said he thought that
Loren's access would be restored in the next couple of
days.

Chapter 3 – Discrimination, Intimidation and Retaliation

Over the next few days, nothing happened.
Benson said little, except to insist that Loren's case was
under review. After several days of reflecting on Jodi's
statements about Loren and myself, I came to believe even
more strongly that racial discrimination was a factor. I
believed it was a factor in Loren's removal from the
laboratory and also in management's refusal to cooperate
with the investigation.

I decided to send an email to Arantza Zabala,
BEA EEO/Employee Relations manager. I asked to meet
with her on May 9. I notified Benson via email. He
responded promptly, letting me know he was disappointed
that I was reporting this matter. He made it clear that he
was unhappy with me alleging that BEA management was
guilty of discrimination.

On May 9, 2005 I met with Zabala. I told her of
Jodi's comments and my opinion that discrimination was a
factor in actions taken with Loren's case. I expressed my
opinion that if Loren had been the "right" race or the right
religion it is likely his access would never have been
revoked. And if it had been, the matter would have been
resolved in days rather than months. I also shared my
concern that my being African American trying to help

another African American, may have led my colleagues to not take the matter seriously. I encouraged Zabala to validate and verify that Loren's treatment was consistent with that of other employees.

I was disappointed, but not surprised by Zabala's reaction to my concerns. She barely took notes and her face was stoic throughout our conversation. Zabala and Jodi had worked issues together for years and were good friends. Jodi's boss was also good friends with Zabala, along with ICP attorneys Dennis Love and Julie Piper.

According to statements from Loren and his union representative, there were other construction workers working at the INL with much more serious and recent violations of the law. I was personally aware of white BEA employees that had criminal records. To validate this I went to the county courthouse and reviewed publically available records. I confirmed that several employees, a couple within BEA Security, had more serious problems with the law than did Loren (since 1998). I forwarded this information to Zabala.

On June 8, 2005, because no action had been taken, I met with Goldman's boss, Cal Ozaki. I informed him of the various procedure violations, potential privacy act violations and potential discrimination. I provided him a written summary. Ozaki seemed vaguely aware of the issues, but knew little of the details. He agreed to review the matter and take appropriate actions.

Nearly four months after I received the call on the Ethics Helpline, Loren's access to the INL was restored. When notified, I slumped in my chair with a deep sigh of relief. The challenge and controversy was worth it.

The following week, Benson and I were sitting in his office discussing the events of the past few months.

"Is BEA going to reimburse Loren for any lost time and wages?" I asked.

"No, we don't have to and we're not going to."

"What about an apology?" Benson glared at me. Defiantly he responded, "Why would anyone apologize?"

At this moment I felt disgust and contempt toward someone whom I used to call my friend.

In early July, Zabala sent me an email note stating that she found no evidence that discrimination was a factor. I was disappointed in the outcome, but not surprised. I had experience, both inside and outside of the INL that told me this decision was not based on facts, but rather what was deemed to be in the best interests of BEA.

Discrimination is a subject I knew up close and personally. In the early nineties, I assisted a family member with a discrimination complaint. This person was the first African American female nuclear operator at the laboratory, perhaps in the nation. She had been involved with a minor release of radioactive water. She acknowledged her mistake but noted that white males had made the same mistake with no disciplinary action taken. In her case, she was suspended without pay for twenty days and a disciplinary letter placed in her file.

She originally filed her discrimination complaint with the company Equal Employment Opportunity office. After an internal investigation, we were told there was no discrimination. Subsequently we filed a complaint with the Idaho Human Rights Commission (IHRC). The IHRC investigation concluded that the suspension was discriminatory and ordered the company to reimburse the monies and provide her with a position in engineering (partly based on issues involving sexual harassment). She would go on to complete her master's degree in engineering and advocate for fairness for female engineers at the laboratory. The lead attorney for the company at this time -- Dennis Love.

In 1993, I was the subject of discrimination, intimidation and threats. I had applied for a management position. I had completed the company manager development program with scores in the 90s and had excellent performance reviews. In spite of being eminently qualified, I wasn't even interviewed.

The EEO office convened a meeting that included the EEO manager, the hiring manager and myself. When I questioned the manager about his selection process, he pointed his finger in my face and yelled, "I'm in your face, man." As he left, he slammed the door. I looked over at the EEO manager and shrugged my shoulders. He sighed and said, "well, I guess we'll find out if the bear shits in the woods." A few days later the threatening manager was disciplined and removed from his position. The job was reposted and I was given the opportunity to interview for the job. Four months later I was selected for my first manager position.

The bottom line is that Zabala failed to provide any facts or evidence that supported her conclusion that there was no discrimination. I didn't believe that her review of this matter was fair and objective.

On July 17, I informed Benson via email that I intended to meet with Laboratory Director, John Grossenbacher and share with him the results of my investigation. Throughout my career, I had always had the opportunity to meet with the president when there were matters that posed a risk to the company. In the past, Benson had supported me.

Later that day, General Counsel Olsen called me.
I told him that in my opinion the actions taken by security,
legal and others made this one of the most egregious acts
of misconduct I'd seen in my tenure as Ethics Officer.
When I shared my intent to meet with Grossenbacher, he
responded, "Do you really want to take me on?"

For a split second I couldn't breathe. I had just
been threatened by one of the most powerful and
influential managers in BEA. After regaining my
composure, I asked him what he meant.

"I will challenge your credibility with
Grossenbacher," he replied.

After taking a deep breath, I said, "I will stand on
my credibility and integrity."

After hanging up, I sent an email to Benson letting
him know that I believed the statement from Olsen was
threatening and intimidating, with the intent of keeping me
from speaking to Grossenbacher.

On Thursday, August 11, at my request, I met
with Juan Alvarez, director of Facilities and Site Services
(Security reported to him), Benson, and Katherine
Moriarty, legal. I presented the facts once again and
provided a written report to Alvarez. We discussed the
security procedure violations, potential privacy action
violations, and the failure of management to cooperate
with the investigation.

At the end of the meeting I stated: "In my opinion
if Loren had filed a discrimination complaint with the

Idaho Human Rights Commission, BEA would have lost."

Alvarez's face turned red as he shoved the report in his folder. "This meeting is over," he declared.

As Benson and I walked backed to our offices he said he was very disappointed in me. I told Benson I felt I had simply reviewed the facts and expressed my opinion.

Ironically, on Sunday I would be leaving to attend three days of *investigative training* at Battelle Memorial corporate headquarters in Columbus, Ohio. I stopped by my office on Friday to finish some work that needed to be completed before my departure. When I opened the door, I found a sealed envelope had been slipped under my door. I opened the envelope and was stunned to see a letter titled, "Response to Findings of Ethics Investigation."

Alvarez had provided a written response less than 24 hours after our meeting. Never before had a written response been provided in such a short time. As I read the letter, I felt like I had made a difference. The first four responses acknowledged a measure of responsibility and accountability. Then came the last bullet. I felt as though I had been shot in the chest.

Alvarez wrote that my comments at the end of the meeting "demonstrated a lack of impartiality unacceptable for someone in his position. This bias and lack of impartiality was interpreted by my staff to be offensive and threatening, no doubt contributing to their measured response to his inquiries."

My hands shook and my heart pounded. It only got worse when I realized the letter was not addressed to me and I was not on distribution.

Obviously, I wasn't supposed to see Alvarez's

letter. The letter was addressed to Benson with copies
sent to Grossenbacher, Lynn Goldman, Arantza Zabala,
Mark Olsen and the Human Resource Director. It was
clear to me that my reputation and career had just been
dealt a severe blow. A senior manager describing the
ethics officer as lacking impartiality and quoting his
managers as saying "I was threatening" was damning to my
credibility and integrity and hence to my career. It was at
this moment that I realized my efforts to do my job to the
best of my ability had resulted in retaliatory actions. I felt
betrayed by the company that I believed was going to lead
the INL to being a world-class laboratory. The words
"valuing and respecting our people" rang hollow in my ears.

I left my office with the letter in my hand. Later
that evening, I shared with LaVonna what had happened.
We both remembered the conversation in early March
when we were worried what might happen if I were to
pursue justice for Loren. Here we sat, several months later
and we had our answer. BEA senior management had put
a target on my back that could destroy my career.

On Sunday, August 14, 2005, I packed and left the
family behind as I headed for the Battelle corporate office
in Columbus. I was attending investigative training from
HR Management Solutions. The most important thing
that I learned from the training is that having an opinion,
and being willing to speak up, is an expectation of the job.

In fact, the instructor said "If you aren't ready to
express an opinion that is contrary to management's, then
you are in the wrong job." She said that when you are
behind closed doors, "you need to have the courage to let
the fur fly."

DENNIS PATTERSON

As I heard this, I understood that a person could only do this if there was a work culture that encouraged open communications and what was often referred to by Grossenbacher as "institutional honesty." I knew that I exhibited courage by expressing an opinion that was contrary to that of senior management, but now I was in the midst of a struggle that could severely impact my future and that of my family.

During the second day of training, the instructor asked for volunteers to role play an incident involving discrimination. I quickly volunteered. An African American female, Demetrei also volunteered. She did a great job portraying a victim of discrimination – and I think I did a good job of playing the role of the investigator of the complaint.

During a break, l took the opportunity to visit with Demetrei. She was intrigued about what it was like to be African American and live in Idaho. I told her about the incident involving Loren. She expressed surprise and outrage that something like this could happen in the year 2005. She mentioned that she was the manager of diversity for Battelle Memorial Institute. As we parted I had no idea that in the not too distant future Demetrei and I would be meeting again. Only this time, it would be much more than role playing.

Chapter 4 – Corporate Governance

During September and October I sent Benson several emails expressing concerns about what had happened to Loren and what I believed was retaliation against me. On September 8, 2005, I sent Benson an email

informing him I had scheduled a meeting with
Grossenbacher to be held in October. Five days later
Benson informed me that Battelle Corporate had decided
to send a team of investigators out to Idaho Falls to
investigate my concerns. My meeting with Grossenbacher
was canceled.

In late October, I received the call. Two
investigators from Corporate wanted to interview me on
November 2. At last, someone from outside BEA was
going to investigate. I was hopeful that justice would
finally prevail and that appropriate corrective actions
would be taken.

I called LaVonna and told her about the
upcoming interview. She expressed optimism that once
corporate understood the facts and realized that I had
risked my career to help BEA do the right thing, I might
be even be rewarded with a position in the corporate office
in Columbus, Ohio. My career would be restored.

I cautioned her that this was perhaps a bit too
much to hope for.

The morning of November 2, my palms were
sweating as I waited outside the office where the
interviews were being conducted. I said a brief prayer and
reviewed my notes. The lead investigator, a corporate
attorney, opened the door and greeted me. I almost
stumbled when I saw Demetrei sitting at the interview
table. I joked about the irony of role playing with her less
than three months ago.

The interview lasted about four hours. At the
conclusion of the interview, I handed Demetrei a summary
of my concerns and issues. They informed me that over

the next couple of days they would be interviewing security personnel as well as Benson, Olsen, Alvarez and others.

Upon returning to work after Christmas break, we learned that one of our colleagues had threatened to kill himself. The morning of January 1, a security guard lay prone on the ground, with his gun pointed at his head. For hours he threatened to pull the trigger. Fortunately, one of the Employee Assistance Program professional counselors was able to intervene and talk him into putting the gun down.

Shortly afterwards, employees reported to me their concern that perhaps the work environment had contributed to the person's mental instability. Specifically, they believed that the transition from the prior contractor to BEA had been handled poorly, resulting in low morale and high stress. I made an appointment with the head of Employee Assistance Program. He assured me that these concerns were being taken seriously. I had no doubt about his sincerity, but I wondered if senior management would take appropriate actions.

On February 10, I met with BEA senior manager Art Clark to review the results of the Battelle corporate investigation. Clark sat at the table with a copy of the report in his hands. He stated that the report did not find any unethical actions, including intimidation or retaliation, on the part of senior management. He further noted they found no evidence of discrimination.

Clark told me that my actions were admirable because I was willing to fight for someone whom no one else seemed to care about. He said Benson should have never taken "no" for an answer when he asked to look at the security file. He went on to say that Benson could never be successful in a line management role because he wasn't strong enough to take the required actions. Clark

said if I had come to him early on, the matter would have
been addressed much sooner. He mentioned that the
corporate investigation concluded that the Ethics Office
was in good shape and things there were going well.

This is when I first learned that Battelle corporate
not only investigated my concerns, they also investigated
me and the effectiveness of the Ethics Office. I was very
distressed to learn this. Had I known I would have
provided additional information and named my own
witnesses for corporate to interview.

At the end of the meeting I said, "Something has
to be done about the Alvarez letter because it has damaged
my reputation and career."

"I will do my best, but I'll need to find a way for
him to save face," Clark responded.

I was heartened that Clark committed to address
the Alvarez letter. But, I was disappointed that none of
the intimidating and threatening actions of BEA senior
management had been acknowledged. Nonetheless, this
was the best I had felt about my career in the past year.
For the first time in many months, I felt like things were
going to work out.

Chapter 5 – It Only Gets Worse

On Friday, February 17, 2006, I went to work
expecting to have a great day. During this time, BEA
management was conducting annual performance reviews.

I was hopeful that in spite of the controversies, I would be recognized and rewarded for overturning the injustice perpetrated toward Loren, protecting the interests of BEA and last but not least, following the INL Standards of Conduct & Business Ethics.

Benson came into my office and sat down at the table. He told me we needed to discuss my performance. He handed me the written appraisal and asked me to read it. I slumped in my chair and let out a sigh of exasperation. I had been penalized for my efforts to help Loren and the discussion with Alvarez. My ratings for the prior seven years were outstanding. This one was two levels lower.

"You know what this looks like," I said.

Benson knew I meant it looked like retaliation. His face turned red and he squirmed in his chair.

I told him that the information I received from Clark was very favorable and that this rating did not reflect that. I also told him that Clark said he would be taking action to address the Alvarez letter. Benson seemed surprised, but said that he would speak to Clark and reconsider the performance appraisal.

One week later, Benson knocked on my door, entered my office and sat down. He held a piece of paper in his hand. With detached coldness and arrogance, he told me that my job title had been changed from manager to specialist. He attempted to justify this action by stating that I did not have anyone directly reporting to me, and therefore I couldn't be a manager. He added that this change in title had the impact of reducing the upper salary range for me by $2,000.

I was taken aback by this blatant and bold act of

retaliation. I knew of several individuals who had no one
reporting to them, but they still retained the "manager"
title. Benson said the change didn't really affect my job title
and told me I could continue to use the manager title on
my INL business cards and other BEA communications.

"You've got to me kidding me – I am not going to
use a title that you just took away," I responded.

Apparently to placate me, Benson was offering me
an option that conflicted with my own sense of honesty
and ethics.

"To use the title would be a misrepresentation and
in my opinion, unethical," I added.

Benson went on to say that he spoke to Clark.
Clark denied making any statement about addressing the
Alvarez letter. I was stunned by these remarks. Either
Clark lied to me, or Benson was lying to me now. BEA
had taken away any hope that my career could be salvaged.
My efforts to resolve these matters within the company
and corporate process had failed.

Chapter 6 – Whistleblower

In early March 2006, I attended the Spring
Conference of the Employee Concerns Program Forum in
Philadelphia. I always looked forward to the conferences.
It was great getting to know folks in similar jobs dealing
with similar challenges. It also was an opportunity to meet
and interface with DOE Employee Concerns

professionals. We always set aside time to share lessons learned and improve our understanding of DOE requirements and regulations.

On the third day of the conference, there was special training offered by Ms. Billie Garde. Billie was an attorney who provided investigation and whistle-blower training to corporations and organizations throughout the country.

I was among the first attendees to sign up. Given what I had endured over the past several months, I wanted to learn as much as possible.

Billie began the training session by sharing her personal story as a former whistle blower. She described a very painful time in her life when she worked for the Census Bureau in Oklahoma. Part of her job was to hire people consistent with the ethnic composition of the region. Over the years, Native Americans had been significantly undercounted. It was important that they, along with other ethnicities, had proper Census Bureau representation.

Unfortunately, the district manager was more concerned about his own political agenda. He directed Billie to hire only those people who would be of benefit to him, who would owe him favors. He went so far as to instruct her to change Civil Service test scores to ensure the right people were hired. He also made sexual overtures to her and told her that the young women she hired had to sleep with local political leaders.

To her credit, Billie had the courage to report this misconduct to the local congressman's office and to the Census Bureau's regional director. Upon learning that she had reported him, her boss then systematically attempted to intimidate her.

He called her into his office and threatened her in a variety of ways and told her to keep her mouth shut about what he was doing. Those threats included interfering with the custody arrangements with her two children. He also spread rumors about her sex life and questioned her fitness as a mother. Finally, after other workers in the office also complained about his sexual exploitation, her boss fired her.

Billie chose to relocate to the East Coast. Soon after arriving she received a call from an Oklahoma newspaper reporter who was writing a story about the Census Bureau scandal. With some trepidation, she agreed to tell what she knew.

After the story appeared, her boss waged a vicious campaign against her by spreading rumors such as being an unfit mother. He attempted to destroy her credibility and reputation in the community. Unfortunately for her boss, these actions only made her more determined to keep fighting. She along with others testified against her ex-boss before a grand jury.

Facing substantial prison time, her former boss pleaded guilty to Conspiracy to Defraud the United States.

Throughout this horrific ordeal, Billie had the strength, courage, determination and conviction to pursue justice to the end. At the age of 30, she enrolled in law school and became the director of the Citizens Clinic for Accountable Government. Several years later she opened her own law practice. Since then, she has been assisting whistle-blowers, especially those in the nuclear industry.

During the presentation, Billie described the profile of someone who would make the ideal whistleblower. The person would need to have an excellent performance history, be well respected in the community, and be a person of great integrity and character. She stated that the person would also have to have the courage and strength to endure the inevitable struggle that would come with being a whistle-blower.

After the training I told her how much I admired and respected her. She thanked me and presented me with a Certificate of Training, "Methods to Detect, Prevent, and Investigate Retaliation in the Workplace" signed Billie Pirner Garde.

As I stared out the window on my flight home, I realized that everything happening in my life had a purpose. God has a purpose for everything and every person. Billie spoke directly to my situation, my character and my heart. I was on my way home with a sense of peace and purpose. Nothing could deter me now. I knew what I had to do.

A few days after my return from Philadelphia, Benson came into my office with a piece of paper in his hand. It was the company form used to document merit increases. I glanced toward the bottom and saw the amount. I was surprised to see that my raise was only slightly less than in past years. Given that my performance appraisal had been substantially lowered it seemed odd that my merit wasn't similarly impacted. Was it a bribe to keep my mouth shut?

Over the next few days, I reflected on the events of the last year. Specifically, my performance appraisal, job title and merit increase. My training and experience told me that the most common method of retaliation was related to performance appraisals and money. I also remained deeply concerned about discrimination and its impact on my career and the Loren case.

What, if any, action was I going to take? Basically, the choices were to do nothing, file a discrimination complaint with the Idaho Human Rights Commission (IHRC), or file a whistle-blower complaint with the Department of Energy. I decided to file an IHRC discrimination complaint.

My prior success filing with the IHRC was the deciding factor, but this was also an opportunity to highlight the need for greater diversity at the Laboratory. There had not been an African American senior manager at the lab, including DOE, since 1999. During Lockheed Martin's tenure (1994-1999) blacks were in prominent positions including General Counsel, VP of Engineering, Executive VP, Diversity Director and Ethics/Employee Concerns. Hispanics and females were also better represented in senior leadership. In late March, I prepared my discrimination complaint and faxed it from my office to the IHRC.

Several weeks later, the IHRC sent me a copy of BEA's rebuttal to my complaint. It was several pages long with the typical legal jargon I'd come to expect. BEA stated that in no way was race a factor or consideration. After reviewing BEA's response, I made the difficult decision to request dismissal of the complaint. I knew that the IHRC generally favored the laboratory and that it would be an uphill struggle to prove discrimination.

In April, I sent an email to the IHRC requesting that they dismiss my complaint of discrimination. Before they would dismiss my complaint I was required to explain why I was making the request. I ended up sending a couple more emails before the IHRC agreed to dismiss my complaint.

At this point, I decided to file a government Code of Federal Regulation 708 "whistleblower" complaint with the U.S. Department of Energy Office of Hearings and Appeals. This was a risky decision. BEA was the major employer in eastern Idaho and Battelle managed five of the nine multiprogramming DOE National Laboratories. I thought, David vs. Goliath part two?

On June 1, 2006, I sent the 708 complaint to Ms. Jan Ogilvie, DOE Idaho Program Manager for Employee Concerns. I had gotten to know Jan over the past several months. We had developed a good working relationship. She was responsible for oversight of the BEA employee concerns office. We both attended the March ECP meeting in Philadelphia.

I stopped by her office to confirm receipt of the complaint. Jan informed me that my complaint would be reviewed by Beth Sellers, Manager of DOE Idaho prior to being sent to Grossenbacher. While I respected Jan, I was concerned that she had no ethics or employee concerns experience prior to assuming this position a few months ago.

Chapter 7 – Injustice Again

A month earlier, on May 1, 2006 a mid-level manager, Kathy stopped by my office. She told me an employee, Eric had spoken to her about an alleged injustice. She expressed her opinion that there was merit to his complaint, but there was nothing she could do. Eric was afraid his manager would retaliate if he reported the issue to Employee Concerns, therefore she was here on his behalf. I explained I couldn't take any action unless Eric came forward.

A few days later, Eric showed up in my office.
His voice quivered and he nervously shifted in his chair.
Eric told me about a disagreement with a manager at the
end of last year. The result of that disagreement, Eric
alleged, was a poor performance appraisal and a
disciplinary action. Eric expressed concern that his
manager would likely retaliate again and perhaps terminate
him if I investigated his allegation. I quoted company
policy against retaliation, but cautioned him that it was no
guarantee. Eric's face went white, but with a sense of
determination he said, "Do it, if it doesn't help me, maybe
it will help someone else."

Over the next few weeks I conducted an extensive
investigation. I interviewed Eric's immediate manager and
next level manager. I also reviewed Eric's performance
appraisal for the prior year. To my surprise, he had
received the highest possible rating, "Outstanding."

In addition, the appraisal contained a hand written
note from the Laboratory Director, "Thank you for your
significant contributions to the success of the lab."

The record showed that three years earlier Eric
was a "Laboratory Fellow." A fellow is the highest
professional designation at INL. This designation meant
that Eric was nationally and internationally recognized in
his area of scientific study. I reviewed written input from
several managers, internal and external to the INL. The
feedback was overwhelmingly positive. I discovered that
the rating Eric received, "does not meet expectations,"
placed him at the very bottom of the laboratory. Only one
other INL employee received this rating and this person

had since been terminated.

The other issue Eric reported was the discipline letter. The letter was largely based on the same information in the performance appraisal, with one exception. It quoted another manager as being disappointed with Eric's performance. When I interviewed the manager she stated she was more than pleased with his performance and in fact would like him to work for her again.

About a month after I began the investigation, Eric stopped by my office. As he stood at the door I could see the burden of stress on his face. He had lost weight since we last met. He was having trouble sleeping, had no appetite and had difficulty concentrating. He told me the investigation was having a similar effect on his wife. I tried to encourage him and apologized for the investigation taking so long. I told him that I too was going through a stressful time and therefore I could understand. As we parted, I told him that what sustained me was my faith, my family and my friends.

It was another couple weeks before I saw Eric again. When he arrived I met him at the door. I could see that he looked better. I sensed a level of peace as he began to speak. He told me that the words I shared with him the last time had made a difference. He could tell I wasn't sure what words he was referring to. He asked me if I remembered what I said.

I somewhat sheepishly told him I didn't. Eric reminded me about my comment regarding faith, family and friends. We gave each other a hug and wished each other well. I told Eric I would keep him updated.

I sat at my desk and pondered my own situation. My stress level was beginning to worry me. I reflected

42

upon a time a few years ago. I had just met with an
employee who had reported an allegation of unfair
treatment. After the person left, my chest started feeling
heavy. I went to the first floor and checked in with the
company doctor. I ended up being carted off to the
hospital in an ambulance. Fortunately, I didn't have a
heart attack, but I was put on blood pressure medication
with instruction to watch my stress level.

I completed the investigation of Eric's complaint
the end of June. The evidence overwhelmingly supported
his allegations. On July 10, 2006 I issued the investigative
report to the senior manager. The report substantiated
Eric's complaint. I reminded Eric's management of BEA's
policy forbidding retaliation when an employee reports
misconduct. I recommended that management reassess
the performance appraisal and the disciplinary action and
take appropriate action.

Within a few days of the issuance of the report, I
was contacted by Eric. He said he believed that he was
being retaliated against for reporting his concerns and for
the report I sent to management.

"They revised my appraisal alright, now it's worse
than before I came to you. The discipline letter was revised
also, but now it has more negative comments. My career
is destroyed," he said.

My heart sank, my efforts had only made matters
worse. Eric tried to fight back the tears. He told me that
he and his family had decided to leave Idaho Falls. "My
family loves Idaho Falls, we don't want to leave, but I'm
left with no choice." Eric noted that he had a couple of
opportunities at two DOE national labs that he was

seriously considering.

"Would you like to file a retaliation complaint," I asked.

"Management would only make my life even more miserable" Eric replied.

"I'm sorry" was all I could say.

I told Eric he had reason to be proud of his contributions to the laboratory. I expressed my regret that BEA management had failed to honor its commitment to fair and ethical behavior. Then, to my surprise Eric said, "Dennis, I will always be thankful for your efforts."

What a gracious and generous response, especially when contrasted with a vengeful and vindictive management team. I would soon learn just how vicious they could be!

Chapter 8 – African American Alliance

In early 2006 a good friend, Dave Snell talked to me about some of the challenges of being African American and living in Idaho. Dave said that he spoke with my brother and he had some of the same concerns. My brother, Donald Patterson, is pastor of Community Church of God in Christ, the oldest predominantly African American church in Idaho Falls.

In April 2006, Dave and I met at my brother's home. We brainstormed how we could contribute to improving diversity and understanding in our community. As we sat at the kitchen table I imagined what it must have

been like in the 50's and 60's as folks met in churches and
pastors' homes during the Civil Rights era.

The following month, we convened a breakfast
meeting at a local restaurant. The meeting was well
attended with passionate discussion about the issues and
how we might address them.

Issues included: limited cultural opportunities,
lack of ethnic products & services, racial intolerance,
employment, and education. A specific concern was the
apparent lack of commitment to diversity at the laboratory,
including DOE Idaho.

We met weekly to formulate our goals, strategies
and mission statement. Coming up with a mission
statement that everyone could support turned out to be an
arduous and sometimes painful process. Finally, we agreed
upon the following, "We are committed to initiating
dialogue and providing resources that contribute to the
educational, cultural and economic future of our
community. And to promote understanding among all
races."

We also struggled with coming up with a name for
our organization. The consensus was that the organization
would be open to everyone and would address a wide
range of diversity issues. However, we also wanted a name
that would recognize the presence and contribution of
African Americans. This was important, in part, because
Blacks make up less than 1% of the population. After
healthy debate we agreed upon the name "African
American Alliance (AAA)."

We scheduled the meeting to elect officers for the
AAA in June 2006. As the time approached I spoke with

LaVonna about my desire to lead the organization. I told her I wanted to be the President. LaVonna was fully supportive but she encouraged me to pray about it before making a final decision. I did so earnestly. On the day of the meeting, I told her that I believed this was the time and this was the opportunity. At the end of the meeting we walked out together arm in arm, I as the president of the African American Alliance and she as my greatest supporter.

I felt humbled and honored to have the opportunity to lead an organization that was committed to improving our community.

Chapter 9 – Religious Freedom

One warm, sunny summer day in July, I returned to my office after visiting a friend in another building. I was having a very routine day when my phone rang. The caller identified himself and said he wanted to report a concern. He told me that he and a couple of other employees had posted flyers on company bulletin boards and that some unknown person had removed them. He said he believed his religious freedom was being compromised.

I asked him why this was a religious matter. He said that several employees had decided to hold a "prayer breakfast" at a local park. The flyer was posted to let all interested employees know about the breakfast.

The purpose was to pray for the welfare of the laboratory and employees. The flyer contained the words "*prayer breakfast*" and provided the date, time and location. He wondered if I could follow up to find out why the

flyers were removed and see if they could be reposted.   I
agreed to do so.

I discovered that the Diversity Office and Legal
Office had decided that it was inappropriate to allow
employees to post information on bulletin boards that
included a reference to prayer. Their position was that
allowing such flyers would give the impression that the
company supported the event. They further reasoned that
it would make non-Christians feel uncomfortable.

I was copied on several emails sent by a friend,
John Howze. John worked in the Communication and
Public Affairs organization. The emails were sent to Legal
and Diversity. John cited several references that, in his
opinion, contradicted the company's position and in fact
suggested it might be illegal for the company to prohibit
the posting of the subject flyers. I then sent emails to
Diversity and Legal wherein I stated my support of John's
position.

After the exchange of several emails between
John, Diversity, Legal, and myself, it became clear that
sending emails was not an effective approach to resolve
this issue. John and I sent emails requesting the
opportunity to meet with Legal and Diversity face-to-face.
We wanted to have open and direct communications and
hopefully come to a resolution acceptable to both sides of
this issue.

To our surprise, General Counsel, Mark Olsen
and the manager of Diversity, Arantza Zabala refused to
sit down and talk to us. They said they would accept
emails from us but were adamant that no face-to-face
discussions would occur. In response to this arrogant

attitude, I sent an email to Benson requesting that he intervene and help facilitate the opportunity to have dialogue about this matter. He refused.

A few days later, John informed me that Legal had contacted his manager and told him John was causing problems and it needed to stop. John and I believed that this was another example of Legal trying to intimidate someone in response to raising a concern. Afraid of being fired, John decided to take no further action.

In the process of pursuing the flyer issue, I decided it would be appropriate to revisit a previous controversial subject. In early 2005, The Post Register ran a front page story about an INL policy that prohibited employees from holding bible studies on laboratory premises. Zabala was quoted as strongly defending the policy and was adamant that no change was forthcoming.

I disagreed with the policy and hence decided to conduct my own research on the matter. I contacted colleagues at other DOE national laboratories and discovered that these laboratories allowed bible studies as long as they were held during lunch or before or after work.

I then sent emails supporting a change in policy to Legal and Diversity. After several weeks of heated debate, Legal and Diversity agreed to change company policy and allow employees to hold bible studies consistent with other laboratories.

The company issued an iNote (an email message that is the standard vehicle for BEA to communicate with the work force) to all employees. The iNote contained good news and bad news. The good news was that holding bible studies on the premises was now acceptable. The policy also allowed for discussion of religion among employees as long as both parties were comfortable. An employee could actually share his/her faith with others without the fear of being in violation of some company procedure or policy. The bad news was that posting anything religious (including reference to prayer) was still prohibited.

Because of the last ruling, the prayer breakfast flyers were never allowed to be posted. In spite of this, the event was held as scheduled. Those of us in attendance prayed for each other, our community and the INL. Over the next year, the prayer breakfast continued as a small, tightly knit weekly prayer meeting held at the homes of INL employees. Prayers regularly went forth for the INL and its employees. I was blessed by meeting fellow Christians and building prayer partners that cared about the INL and about me.

Chapter 10 - Persecution

June 2006 was an interesting month. I became the president of AAA and I filed a DOE whistleblower complaint. Both events would turn out to be defining moments in my life.

I never thought about becoming a whistleblower. During my years as the Ethics Officer/Employee Concerns Manager, I had helped the company defend itself against whistleblowers. I knew that the journey of a whistleblower was long, arduous, painful and expensive. I knew that in most cases, if not all, it was a death knell to the whistleblower's career.

My personal burden had become heavy and the stress sometimes seemed unbearable. Already I had received an unfair performance appraisal, been demoted, and my reputation had been damaged by the Alvarez letter. Now, I was worried that BEA would take even more drastic actions based on the fact that I filed the complaint with DOE. LaVonna's biggest worry was my health. As a psychologist she knew the emotional and physical damage that could result from long term high stress.

On Thursday, July 13, 2006, my day began as usual. It was a beautiful sunny morning. I poured myself a steaming hot cup of coffee and went out on the deck for some quiet time before leaving for work. As I sat there, Ziggy, our black playful cocker spaniel, jumped in my lap. I stroked her soft coat as she licked my face. I was thankful to have a beautiful home and a loving family. Before leaving for work, I gave LaVonna a kiss and she said, "Have a great day."

I was at work sitting at my computer at work when the phone rang.

"My name is Torrance, I'm an investigator with BEA Security. I need to meet with you in a half hour, in my office," the deep voice boomed with authority.
My heart pounded and I could hardly breathe as I realized I was being investigated.

"Why do you need to meet with me," I said after catching my breath.

"I can't tell you why."

"Look, I am a trained investigator and I know you can tell me if you want to," I said.

"OK, you are under investigation for misuse of government equipment."

My gut wrenched and my head felt like it was
going to explode. Composing myself, I responded, "I will
be down to your office in 30 minutes, maybe sooner."

My trembling hand dropped the receiver back in
its cradle. This was unreal. It felt like the beginning of a
horrible nightmare. Without even thinking about it, I
knew that this was retaliation. BEA had found out about
my whistleblower complaint just ten days ago and now I
was being investigated for the first time in my 26 year
career.

For several minutes I sat there, trying to calm
myself. I prayed, "God please protect me, please help me
prepare for what is coming, give me the strength and
courage to persevere, allow me to face this with dignity
and humility." I knew that I had not misused government
equipment or time, but I also knew that being innocent
doesn't always mean you won't be found guilty. Innocent
people have been fired from their jobs, innocent people
have been persecuted, sent to jail, even put to death. Yes,
I was innocent, but I needed to do everything I could to
protect myself and my family.

I arrived at Torrance's office 25 minutes after his
call. He reiterated that he was asked to investigate me for
misuse of government time and equipment. At the
beginning of the interview, he told me it would be best if I
told him the truth. He then turned on a recording device
and placed it on the table.

"Dennis, have you ever misused government
equipment?"

"Absolutely not, I want to know who has accused
me of this."

"Management requested that I investigate you, but that's all I can tell you." "Have you ever received or sent personal emails from your work computer?" he asked.

"Of course I have, as allowed by company policy."

"Give me some examples."

"I sometimes communicate with family and I have communicated with members of the African American Alliance. Company policy allows me to send the emails related to the African American Alliance for two reasons. First, it only took a few minutes of time and second, the AAA mission supports the diversity initiative of the company."

"Anything else?" Torrance asked.

"Yes, I sent emails to the Idaho Human Rights Commission requesting the dismissal of my discrimination complaint and to DOE regarding my whistleblower complaint."

When I provided this information, his eyes opened wide, he sat up in his chair and leaned towards me, his arm muscles tensed. His body movements reminded me of an animal that had his prey cornered with no way to escape.

Of course, things often aren't what they seem.

"Torrance, you may not know this, but company policy allows me to use time and equipment to file both my discrimination complaint and the whistleblower complaint."

Torrance's face went blank and he leaned back in his chair. It was like the air suddenly escaping from a balloon.

After regaining his composure he targeted my actions related to my whistleblower complaint.

"Did you prepare the whistleblower complaint on your work computer and if so, how much time did you spend," he asked.

I calmly and respectfully replied, "Yes, I charged approximately four hours of time. Torrance, you may not know it but doing so was completely within DOE regulations.

Again, Torrance slumped back in his chair. This interview hadn't gone as he had planned, or had been told it would go.

Torrance closed his notebook and turned off the recording device.

"Dennis, when I complete my investigation I will provide a report to management and they will determine if there will be any disciplinary action…thank you for being cooperative, you know it's not uncommon for the interviewee to be combative…I appreciate the fact that you have been forthright and cooperated fully."

"Torrance, you are just doing your job," I responded. We shook hands as I left his office.

Returning to my office, I needed the soft comforting voice of LaVonna. I took a couple of deep breaths. I knew I was innocent but struggled with the idea of calling and telling her I was under investigation. Finally, I placed the call. She answered, "Hi, Babe, you having a good day?"

"No, sweetheart, I don't even know how to say this...I am being investigated by Security for misconduct...this could lead to my termination."

"I love you," she said. "I believe that you have done nothing wrong...God will see us through this. I will see you when you get home."

Misuse of government equipment was a termination offense. I knew that I needed to respond immediately. I reviewed all the emails I had sent and received since January. Out of the 950 or so emails, I counted 40 that were not work-related. I also calculated an estimate of the amount of time I had spent writing and/or reading the emails related to the discrimination complaint and my whistleblower complaint.

At the end of the day, I sent an email to Torrance and his boss, Tom Middleton. I let them know that my actions were clearly within company policy and DOE regulations. I forwarded the same emails to Legal. It was imperative that I get this information into the appropriate hands right away.

Later, I solicited input from other members of BEA management on the issue of spending time writing the whistleblower complaint. I knew that this would likely be the issue that could lead to my termination. The fact that I admitted to spending several hours of time could be misinterpreted to be time card fraud. Three members of management wrote emails to me stating that writing a DOE whistleblower complaint on company time and equipment was acceptable. They cited company policy and DOE Orders. Upon receiving these emails I forwarded them to Torrance, Middleton, Benson and Olsen.

Within a couple of hours, Olsen sent me an email
stating it was against company policy for me to write my
whistleblower complaint on my work computer. To me,
this was simply an extreme example of arrogance and a
refusal to admit he was wrong. I responded to his email
with quotes from DOE regulations.

Within the hour I received an email from a DOE-
Idaho attorney, a colleague of Olsen's. In the email, she
strongly supported Olsen's wrongheaded position. She
wrote, "In my personal opinion, an employee who files a
complaint against his or her employer (in any industry)
should not be using company time to pursue the
complaint, which must be done on the employee's
personal time." This attorney was missing something very
important. The INL was not just "any industry," it was a
DOE laboratory, operating in accordance with DOE
regulations. Ironically, this attorney would later be
promoted to the senior executive management team of
DOE-ID.

In my opinion, it was totally inappropriate and
improper for a DOE attorney to send me this email. It
suggested to me that DOE could not fulfill its obligation
to provide independent oversight of BEA. It had only
been a couple weeks since I filed my whistleblower
complaint. DOE-Idaho was already taking the side of
BEA.

Although I was sure that I had done no wrong, I
decided to solicit one more opinion. I wrote to the BEA
manager responsible for ensuring compliance with the
INL/DOE Contract. I received the following reply,
"Dennis, In as much as the requirements for filing a
complaint under the Whistleblower Act are included in the

BEA contract and as long as the time charged for completing the form is reasonable, the time an employee uses to write his/her complaint is an allowable cost under the contract. Use of contractor phone and e-mail on company time to complete the complaint in accordance with the contract requirements is also an allowable cost." I forwarded this email to Olsen, Benson, and Moriarty.

During the next several weeks, I heard nothing more on this subject. I feared that each day I went to work could be my last. There were moments of overwhelming despair and anguish, but I never lost hope. I knew that even if I was terminated, I would still have my faith, my family and my friends.

Chapter 11 – Faith and Friendship

During this time of turmoil and uncertainty in my work life, I was also experiencing uncertainty about my church life. Since childhood, I had attended the same church, but now I was feeling a need to make a change. I came to believe that our family would benefit from attending a larger church with youth programs and more opportunities for growth and development.

LaVonna and I prayed about this for weeks before deciding to visit a couple of churches. The second church we visited was the First Church of the Nazarene. When the associate pastor began his message, he asked the congregation to turn to a specific passage in the Bible. The scripture was Acts 14:22...."They encouraged the believers to continue in the faith, reminding them that we must suffer many hardships to enter the Kingdom of God." This was the exact passage that I had bookmarked

in my bible. I had read this passage just yesterday. At the
end of his sermon the Associate Pastor asked for anyone
going through hardship to stand up. LaVonna and I stood
up along with a handful of others. Several church
members came over and prayed for us. At the end of the
service LaVonna and I knew that God had answered our
prayers. We had found our new home church.

There were two other scriptures that provided me
with hope and encouragement. Proverbs 10: 9: "The
man of integrity walks securely, but he who takes a
crooked path will be found out."

And Romans 5:3-5: "We rejoice in our sufferings
because sufferings produce perseverance, perseverance
character, character hope. Hope will not disappoint us;
the Lord will pour out his love through the Holy Spirit."

On the evening of Wednesday, August 27th our
home phone rang. On the other end was a friend who
called to let me know that a dear friend of mine, Americus
John-Lewis (AJ) was in critical condition at the local
hospital. AJ was one of the few people with whom I had
shared my recent troubles. He had been a big supporter,
encourager and confidant. A few years ago when AJ was
president of the local National Association for the
Advancement of Colored People (NAACP), he asked me
to serve as the Legal Redress officer. He and I had dealt
with several discrimination incidents in our community.

The next morning I called in to work to let them
know I would not be in the office because I needed to be
with a friend at the hospital.

I entered the hospital and rode the elevator to the
intensive care unit. The ICU was a controlled area and I

had to press a button and identify myself prior to entering. The door opened and I walked down the hallway to AJ's room. Even lying in bed, AJ was an imposing figure. His six foot nine inch, nearly 300 pound frame seemed to barely fit the bed.

As I entered his room I saw his wife, Catherine; his son Kevin and his daughter Jennifer. I could see the sadness in their eyes and the grief on their faces. AJ was hooked up to life-saving devices and appeared to be in a deep sleep. Catherine greeted me with a smile. I approached AJ, leaned over, squeezed his hand and told him I loved him.

Throughout the morning I stayed with AJ and the family. While I was there, the doctor came into the room. The news wasn't good, but the doctor gave the family hope. Just before lunch, LaVonna stopped by to see AJ. She came in and gave everyone a big hug and words of encouragement. A little later, I remembered something at work that required my immediate attention. Even though I didn't want to leave, I told Catherine I would return shortly.

When I got to my desk, the first thing I did was log onto my computer to check my email. My heart jumped when I saw an email from Torrance, the security investigator. The email said he needed to interview me again and that he wanted to do it later this afternoon. I remembered the phone call from Torrance several weeks ago (July 13) when I was investigated for misuse of government equipment. Was I being investigated again? I replied and let him know I was on personal leave and would get back with him later to schedule the interview.

I returned to the hospital. Around 3:00 p.m. my cell phone rang. It was Torrance.

"Dennis, I need to interview you again. I need to
ask you some follow-up questions...and there is
something else I need to talk to you about."

I was upset about getting this call after telling
him via email that I was on personal leave.

"So, have I been accused of some other
misconduct, am I being investigate again," I asked.

"Dennis, has somebody told you there is another
allegation against you," he asked.

No one had told me anything, but his answer
confirmed my suspicion. I decided to defer answering his
question. I responded, "I'd rather not answer that
question."   At the end of the call I told Torrance I would
call him back after my return to work and schedule the
interview.

Later, this rather brief and seemingly innocuous
phone conversation would be a major issue that BEA
would use to justify taking further retaliation against me.
However, at the moment I didn't care. A close friend of
mine might be dying. Furthermore, LaVonna and I were
leaving the next morning to visit her son, James Williams,
in Fargo, North Dakota. The interview with Torrance
would have to wait.

I stayed at the hospital until late afternoon. When
it was time to leave, I explained to the family that LaVonna
and I would be flying out the next morning to visit her
son. We apologized for leaving at this time, but noted it
had been planned for a couple months. We told them we

would call to see how AJ was doing. I knew as I left the room that this might be the last time I would see him.

The next day, LaVonna and I arrived at the Fargo airport and rented a car. As we drove into the parking lot of the hotel, LaVonna's cell phone rang. We looked at each other as she handed me the phone. On the other end was AJ's son, Kevin. I knew it was bad news. His father had just died.

I don't remember what I said, but I remember Kevin thanking me for being a good friend to his dad. Tears welled up in my eyes as I felt the loss of a dear friend. LaVonna leaned over and held me as she gently kissed my cheek. We prayed for the family.

LaVonna and I enjoyed our visit with her son. It was good for me to see the love between them. James was a member of the National Guard and had returned from Iraq just in time for our wedding in May, 2004. They hadn't seen each other since then.

AJ's funeral service took place the day after our return. The family asked me to say a few words and I was honored to do so. It was a beautiful service with many people from the community including the mayor and other community leaders.

On September 2, 2006, the Post Register's front page headline proclaimed "Local Activist Dies." The article was an excellent tribute to the impact AJ had on our community. My favorite part of the article was a quote from AJ, "I really believe that through love and prayer, we can overcome obstacles. It doesn't matter how high it is. If we want to, we can overcome."

Chapter 12 – Bias

My attention turned to my upcoming interview
with Torrance. At this point I had zero trust in the system.
I was convinced that Torrance was now part of an
institutionalized effort to retaliate against me for filing my
whistleblower complaint.   At my request, BEA agreed to
allow my attorney, DeAnne Casperson to be present
during the interview. I went over and over in my mind
trying to figure out what I had been accused of this time.

It had been almost two months since I was
investigated for misuse of government equipment and I
still didn't know the outcome. I knew that if Legal
maintained it was inappropriate for me to write my
whistleblower complaint on my computer I would likely be
terminated.

On September 5, I sent an email to Olsen and
Katherine Moriarity (lead attorney) and asked what they
had decided.

The morning of the interview, September 6, 2006
I awoke early taking time to read my bible and pray for
God's protection. LaVonna gave me a kiss and said, "I
will be praying for you, God will be with you."

I arrived at work and began preparing for the
interview with Torrance. A couple hours before the
interview, I received an email from Katherine Moriarty. It
was a response to the inquiry I had sent yesterday. Legal
finally made the right decision. It was within policy for me
to write my whistle blower complaint on my work
computer. I was relieved, but disturbed that it took almost

two months for Legal to make a decision that should have taken a couple of hours. And for them to wait until just a few hours before this interview to inform me was wrong. I suspected they waited in order to increase the pressure and anxiety. In fact, if I hadn't sent the email inquiring about the decision I may not have been informed at all.

It was mid-afternoon and time to go down to Torrance's office and be interrogated once again. I sat at my desk and said a prayer before meeting DeAnne in the lobby of the Willow Creek building. We speculated as to what I had been accused of this time. Neither of us could come up with anything. Finally we walked together to Torrance's office.

As we sat down, Torrance turned on his tape recorder.

"Dennis, as you know, you are required to cooperate with this investigation," he began.

He informed me that the new allegation against me was filed by Eric's manager. It was the same manager that I had found guilty of unfair treatment just two short months ago. Management had retaliated against Eric for filing his complaint and now they were retaliating against me. They had filed a complaint with Legal that I had been biased in my investigation of Eric's allegation against them.

I now knew just how vicious Eric's management team could be. I also surmised that Olsen and Benson fully supported this action.

Torrance began the questioning by asking about the first allegation, misuse of government equipment. I asked him if he had seen the email from legal that stated writing my whistle blower complaint on my work computer was not a violation of policy. Torrance said he hadn't, so I handed him a copy.

He then asked, "Has anyone told you that there
was another allegation filed against you?

"No, I replied.

"So, why did you refuse to answer this question
when we talked on the phone?'

I laughed and responded, "I wanted to keep you
guessing, and kind of level the playing field."

He chuckled and proceeded with his questioning.
He focused on the report I had issued to Eric's
management. I explained the process and protocols I used
in conducting the investigation. The interview lasted
approximately ninety minutes.

After leaving the interview, DeAnne and I
discussed how it went. We expressed our disbelief that I
was being investigated by Security for alleged bias.

DeAnne said I handled myself very well. I told
her I was convinced that the two investigations were in
direct response and retaliation for my filing the whistle
blower complaint in June of 2006. What made matters
worse was the fact that the security organization was
performing the investigations. The same organization I
had found guilty of misconduct in the Loren site access
matter in 2005. The conflict of interest couldn't be more
obvious.

Chapter 13 – Conferences

I was scheduled to attend the fall Employee Concerns Program Conference in Indianapolis, Indiana. Ironically, I would be representing BEA as the Employee Concerns Program manager on the heels of just having been investigated twice in the past few weeks. I left on September 11, 2006.

The third day of the conference included a break out session with DOE and DOE Contractor ECP professionals. During the session we shared lessons learned, best practices and significant issues. During the round table discussion I mentioned that after two months of deliberation, BEA senior management decided an employee could use his/her computer to file a whistleblower complaint. The consensus was that doing so was acceptable. Many expressed surprise that this was even debatable.

I chose not to tell them I had filed a whistle blower complaint. However, later in a private discussion with Billie Garde, I shared with her pertinent details of my complaint, specifically that I had been investigated twice over the past two months.

"Dennis, it's hard to believe any company would do this, but I tell you this, I'll be shocked if they decide to terminate you." Billie said.

We spoke for over an hour. It felt good to have the support and encouragement of someone that knew what I was going through. At the end of our conversation she gave me her business card which I tucked away in my wallet.

Upon returning from the conference, I decided to

file an addendum to my whistleblower complaint. On
September 19, 2006 it was filed. I alleged that BEA
management had initiated the two investigations of me in
retaliation for filing my whistle blower complaint.

As September wound to a close I was looking
forward to my next business trip. On October 3, 2006 I
drove to Salt Lake City, Utah for the annual Ethics Officer
Conference. On the second day of the conference there
was a speaker that really grabbed my interest. He spoke
about the challenges of being an Ethics Officer. One
comment he made I have never forgotten, "Anyone who is
or wants to be an Ethics Officers should be prepared to be
fired. There are times when senior management doesn't
want to hear the message, the messenger often becomes
the scapegoat."

Chapter 14 – Day of Judgment

It was Monday, October 16, 2006. I sat at my
computer with the door to my office slightly ajar. At
approximately 3:30 p.m., a shadow appeared in the
doorway. The door swung open and Benson walked in. I
glanced up and saw a document in his hand. My heart
stopped. I knew that I was about to be disciplined.

Benson grabbed a chair from the round table and
placed it directly in front of my desk. He had a look of
arrogance and coldness. The time had come.

"Dennis, you have been found guilty of serious
misconduct," he said. He shoved the discipline letter in

65

front of me. In bold letters was, "SUSPENSION WITHOUT PAY."

Benson read aloud the first paragraph, "Your failure to cooperate with an investigation by misleading an investigator; refusal to answer investigation questions regarding the unauthorized use of government computers and systems and the attendant inferred unauthorized use of government computers and systems; failure to follow company policies and protocols regarding an Employee Concerns investigation; failure to follow directions from BEA Office of General Counsel."

I sat there in horror and disbelief. I looked Benson in eye and said nothing. I knew that words would be futile.

Benson slowly rose to his feet, "Your suspension begins now, let's go."

I took a deep breath. On the wall next to my computer hung a sheet of paper that contained bible scriptures and quotes from Dr. Martin Luther King. I read aloud, "The man of Integrity walks securely, but he who takes a crooked path will be found out."

Benson followed closely behind as I walked down to the guard station near the front entrance. He took my badge, cell phone and the key to my office.

"I'll see you back here at the end of your suspension," he said.

It felt as though I was having an out of body experience. I was watching someone be unjustly persecuted and humiliated. As I crossed the bridge heading to my car the feeling of betrayal was overwhelming. I sat in my car for what seemed like hours,

but was probably just a few minutes. I prayed that God
would help me through this.

I called LaVonna and let her know what had
happened.

"I love you and God loves you, we'll get through
this," she said with the confidence of her unwavering faith.

Chapter 15 – Reflection

The first day of my suspension LaVonna and I flew to
North Carolina to visit her daughters Val Brunson, Patricia
Williams, and her mother, Valderia Brown. LaVonna had
purchased the airline tickets earlier in the summer.

When we arrived in New Bern, NC it was a beautiful
fall day. While LaVonna was busy with family, I drove out
to the Sheraton Hotel where we were married May 22,
2004. I sat and looked upon the gazebo where we
exchanged our vows. I gazed out upon the marina where
the boats were docked and the water was still. LaVonna
and I had been married less than a year when the
challenges of work life began intruding into our marital
and family life.

In spite of everything, I was thankful for a wife who
was loving, supportive and who prayed for me and with
me. Darius and Jasmine brought joy to my life every day.
I was also blessed with my North Carolina family. I had
developed a close and loving relationship with my new
family. Aside from Val, Patricia and "mom" I had a son in

law Emanuel (Val's husband) and a bright, handsome grandson, Isaiah.

This time of reflection provided comfort and encouragement at a time when it was most needed. I knew that the journey of being a whistleblower had just begun and I would need the love of family and friends more than ever. This time also afforded me the opportunity to decide what actions I needed to take in the near term.

Upon returning to work, I met Benson at the guard desk. The smirk on his face told me all I needed to know about the things to come. For the next few months I was required to meet with him weekly to review my progress. I did everything that was outlined in my discipline letter. As such, the meetings went fairly well. Benson appropriately noted my good performance. However, he couldn't hide the disdain that he seemed to harbor for me. He looked for every opportunity to question and challenge my performance. He just couldn't find anything.

A couple weeks after my return I filed another addendum to my whistleblower complaint. I alleged that the suspension without pay was another act of retaliation.

The rest of the year was pretty uneventful. I performed a very thankless job to the best of my ability. All of my colleagues in the Internal Audit organization knew that I had been disciplined and been given time off without pay. They also knew that I had filed the whistleblower complaint. In spite of this, they remained my friends and regularly stopped by my office to visit and provide words of encouragement.

Chapter 16 – Another Tragic Beginning

The beginning of 2007 had an eerie and tragic
similarity to 2006. A colleague was reported missing. A
couple of days later we learned that in the early morning
hours she had parked her car along the Snake River green
belt and walked out onto the partially frozen river. It
wasn't long before the ice broke and she fell into the sub-
freezing waters. She wouldn't have survived long before
succumbing to the frigid temperatures. A cloud of sadness
enveloped the INL as employees learned that a
colleague/friend had apparently taken her own life.

Almost immediately, employees reported concerns
that perhaps the work environment had contributed to her
decision to end her life. The suicide had occurred during
the midst of the employee performance appraisal process.
Some employees speculated that perhaps she had received
a bad review from her manager and this had been the
tipping point in an already stressful life.

I sent an email to the Director of Safety and
Health and encouraged her to consider this possibility. I
didn't know if I had done enough but at least I'd done
something. Later in a video address to all employees
Grossenbacher stated, *"Now I don't know the extent to which
job related stress was a factor in Kathy's death – we probably never
will – but we owe it to her and one another to talk about it openly
and take effective steps as individuals, leaders, and managers to
acknowledge and manage stress in the workplace."*

Chapter 17 – Inaugural Dr. King Banquet

On January 20, 2007, the AAA hosted the first annual MLK banquet at the Shilo Inn. Our keynote speaker was Dr. Walter Massey, President of Morehouse University. Just a few months prior, Morehouse was selected as the keeper of thousands of Dr. King's papers. Dr. Massey had once been the Laboratory Director for Argonne National Laboratories. Argonne National Laboratory West was located near Idaho Falls and as a result Massey had visited Idaho Falls several times during the 1990's.

Mayor Jared Fuhriman opened the event with remarks and welcomed the more than 250 attendees. It was a wonderful evening. Ladies were dressed in their finest and men dressed in everything from tuxedos to Levis (this is Idaho).

Dr. Massey gave a keynote address that was historical and memorable. His speech was titled "A New Look at Dr. Martin Luther King Jr.: A Formula for Social Change in the 21st Century." During his address he stated, "Because it is a fairly, but not exclusively, homogeneous racial, ethnic, and religious community, Idaho Falls has quite a number of opportunities to demonstrate the quality of empathy. There are minorities in this community – African American, Native Americans, and Hispanics to be sure. Members of the Mormon Church, although not a minority here, are minorities in America, as a whole. No doubt, they have had to endure prejudice in the face of ignorance about their religious beliefs, just as other minorities have had to endure prejudice in the face of ignorance about their racial and ethnic identities."

Dr. Massey went on to say, "We can be assured

that from an evolutionary perspective, Dr. King's ideas
apply to our time, just as they did to his. And, we can
honor him best by taking on the challenge he left us to
educate, engage, empathize and effect a world's house that
one day will be the kind of house that everyone can call
home."

As I left the banquet, arm in arm with LaVonna, I
felt honored and privileged to be a part of an event that
was a tribute to my hero, Dr. Martin Luther King Jr.

Chapter 18 – Black History

On February 12, LaVonna and I traveled to
Charleston, South Carolina. I attended the spring meeting
of the Employee Concerns Program Forum. The final day
of the conference included a breakout session which
included only DOE and DOE Contractor ECP
professionals. Present were individuals from the DOE
Office of Hearings and Appeals (OHA). It was likely that
at least one or two of them were familiar with my whistle
blower complaint. OHA was the office conducting the
investigation of my complaint against BEA. There were
times when it seemed someone wanted to ask me a
question or make a comment, but no one ever did.

Being in Charleston during Black History month
was a very positive experience. In the news and around
the community there were acknowledgements and tributes
to the contributions Blacks have made throughout
America's history.

Upon my return from Charleston I contacted BEA's Diversity Office to see if they were going to acknowledge Black History Month. It had been a few years since the Laboratory had recognized the month, even though they regularly recognized other designated months such as National Hispanic Heritage. To my delight, the Diversity Office asked me to write an article. I agreed, but on the condition that the acknowledgment go out under the signature of Grossenbacher. They agreed. I decided to write about the contributions African Americans had made to the Idaho National Laboratory.

Chapter 19 – Opportunity Denied

On March 7, 2007, I received an email from BEA senior manager, Tom Harrison. He asked if I was interested in being the Ombudsman for INL. I responded affirmatively, but told him Benson would have to approve. Tom replied back, "Dennis, you made my day, and not because you have agreed to 'entertain the thought,' but because you would be perfect for the position, especially with your current position here at the INL. Following your conversation with Doug and assuming he is okay with discussing this further, I will make myself available whenever you want to sit down and talk."

This was a part-time job helping to resolve complex issues involving technology transfer and research and development. I could have easily assumed the duties along with my current job. Unfortunately, Benson refused to allow me to accept this new career enhancing opportunity. In my opinion this was another blatant act of retaliation.

Chapter 20 – Confidentiality

The morning of March 22, 2007, Benson told me he had scheduled a meeting for us that afternoon. When I entered his office, I was surprised to see the manager of Security, Joan. Benson began the meeting by discussing a case that I had turned over to Security more than three months ago. The case involved a BEA employee who allegedly was conducting political activity on company time. I found it odd that this was the topic, because I had presumed the case had been resolved and closed some time ago.

I couldn't believe what came next.

"Dennis, you must disclose the name of the employee who reported the allegation," Joan said.

I had never before been asked to disclose the name of a confidential reporting party. My temples began to throb and my chest felt heavy. I tried to explain why disclosing the person's name was wrong and how doing so would damage employee trust.

"You have to understand, I told the employee I would honor the request for confidentiality. I gave the person my word."

Benson's body stiffened. His clenched teeth seemed to grind.

Joan's face turned red and her eyes bulged. She leaned toward me as if to intimidate me.

"Tell us the name. You don't have a choice!" she responded.

"I have never done so before and I don't intend to now," I said.

We spent the several minutes going back and forth. Benson and Joan continued to demand I disclose the name. I continued to defend my right and obligation to maintain confidentiality.

The person accused of conducting political activity was a former State Legislator with significant influence in the community and the state. Because of this, the confidential source wanted to remain anonymous. Bad things sometimes happened to employees that reported misconduct.

The next day I sent Benson an email. I reiterated my belief that it was wrong to disclose the name. I wanted to ensure there was no ambiguity about what he and Security were asking me to do and what my position was.

Chapter 21 – City Government

A few days later, there was a newspaper article that described concerns with the grievance process for Idaho Falls municipal employees. I sent an email to the mayor and offered my advice and counsel. On April 4, 2007, Mayor Fuhriman invited me to his office to discuss the concerns. The process required employees to go through their line manager in order to raise an issue or concern. There was no other path to resolve employee issues. I told the mayor that, in my opinion, such a process was fundamentally unfair to the employees and

created the likelihood that serious city problems might go
unreported. I suggested that employees be provided an
alternative reporting path. The mayor then invited the
City Council president into his office. She was adamant
that the grievance process was effective and didn't need to
be changed. She seemed to take offense that anyone
would question how the city does business.

At the close of the meeting the mayor said,
"Dennis I would like you to review the city's grievance
procedure and provide feedback. I will get a copy to you."

We said goodbye with a firm handshake. I was
confident that the city would revise its procedure so that
employees would have a more fair opportunity to resolve
their issues and concerns and/or to report misconduct.

I never heard back from the mayor and to my
knowledge nothing ever changed. But, at least the mayor
was willing to have the conversation. I hoped this might
prompt changes in the future.

Chapter 22 – Threat and Intimidation

On April 10, 2007 Benson sent me an email. He
stated that it was my obligation to find a resolution to
Security's demand that I release the confidential name.
Over the next few days, I contacted friends and colleagues
with experience in the field of Employee Concerns and
Ethics. I called a friend at a DOE National Laboratory
back east. She informed me that there was only one
occasion where she had been asked to disclose

confidentiality. She told me that in retrospect she shouldn't have done so, but management had convinced her it was ok. She told me she would never do it again.

I also contacted Dan Robertson, Director of Employee Concerns for the INL cleanup contractor (ICP). Dan told me that in his more than twenty five years of conducting investigations and managing employee concerns he had only been asked to break confidentiality once. He said he never disclosed the identity without the knowledge and/or approval of the employee.

Dan helped me develop three viable options to offer in response to the Benson email. The options included: 1) Security provide me with the questions they needed answered and I would ask them of the employee 2) Let me ask the employee if he/she would allow me to release his/her name or meet with security 3) Refer the matter to BEA senior management inclusive of Art Clark and/or Grossenbacher. In Dan's and my opinion, these options would allow Security to move forward with their investigation without damaging the integrity of the Employee Concerns/Ethics Office.

That evening I spoke to LaVonna about the options.

She responded, "Dennis, I don't believe this will satisfy them. I don't even think this is the real issue…they are just trying to intimidate and threaten you."

After a restless night's sleep I awoke knowing what I had to do. I told LaVonna that I could not in good conscience disclose the name of the employee. "I trust your decision, my love," she said as I left for work.

Upon arriving at work, I sent Benson an email. I informed him that I would not release the name. I

communicated the three options that I believed would
assist Security in their investigation. I hoped that reason
would prevail and this ugly situation would come to an
end. However, I couldn't help but think that LaVonna
was probably right. This really wasn't about disclosing the
confidential name.

Chapter 23 – Betrayal

For several days, there was no response to my
email. I only saw Benson occasionally, but we never
spoke, not even, "hello." I was getting very little sleep
and I had lost my appetite. Sometimes just walking down
the hall was exhausting.

Finally, on April 16, I was summoned to a meeting
in Benson's office. Attending were Benson and Tom
Middleton, director of INL Security. Tom was also my
neighbor and someone I considered a friend. In fact, in
1998 he had testified at my divorce hearing. During the
child custody phase, he testified that he knew me well, that
our children were best friends, that I was a good parent,
and a person of integrity.

Over the years, our children had spent countless
hours playing at our home and at Tom's home. Tom and I
shared beers together and had even gone trick or treating
with the kids together. Yet, here we were sitting in
Benson's office on opposite sides of the table and
apparently on opposite sides of a serious BEA conflict.

My supposed friend began the meeting, "Dennis,

you must and will tell my investigator, Dyanna, the name of the employee." For the next several minutes Tom pontificated about the responsibility and authority of the Security organization.

Benson chimed in, "Dennis, it is your obligation to tell Security the name."

I was alarmed by their arrogance and sense of absolute authority. I had no doubt they had already obtained the concurrence and approval of Legal and Human Resources.

As they spoke, I just listened and watched.

Finally, I responded, "Tom, you know me, you know I will not violate my professional or personal ethics." I continued, "Tom, your investigators don't understand BEA or DOE policies, if they did they wouldn't be asking for me to disclose the name."

As I spoke, Middleton's face slowly turned red, his hands and muscles tensed.

"My investigators know what they are doing and you will give us the name," he demanded.

"Dennis, I'm with Tom on this," Benson interjected.

"So, are you directing me to disclose the name," I asked.

Benson replied, "I'm not directing you to but you have an obligation to help Security proceed with the investigation.

I walked out of the office. Tears welled up in my eyes, my head throbbed, and my chest felt heavy as I made my way back to my office.

As LaVonna said, "this really wasn't about
releasing the name of the employee."

On April 24, I was again called into a meeting
with Benson and Middleton. Benson shoved a letter in
front of me. Benson referred to the last page, "You have
until 9:00 a.m. tomorrow morning to provide the name of
the employee."

I sat there in disbelief. In spite of my efforts to
find a workable solution, BEA was forcing me to violate
confidentiality. To make matters worse I was being given
less than 24 hours to make a career and life changing
decision.

I looked across the table at Benson and
Middleton, "Both of you know me well enough to know
what I am going to do." As I rose to leave, my heart was
pounding as though it would come through my shirt.

I paused in the doorway, turned, and looked at
Middleton. Through clenched teeth I said, "You're doing
a great job as Security Director." Little did I know that
this comment would later come back to haunt me.

I returned to my office and prepared an email to
Grossenbacher and other senior managers. I needed to get
them to understand the gravity of this situation. I was
trying to save my job and at the same time keep the
company from doing something that could damage

employee and public trust. At 8:34 p.m. I hit the send key. As I turned off my computer and closed the door to my office I knew this could be one of the last times I would be able to call this "my office."

Chapter 24 – The Decision

The drive home seemed to take forever. It was as though everything was in slow motion. My emotions were running rampant as my thoughts raced and my body reacted to the stress and duress of the day. As I pulled into the garage, I looked in the rearview mirror and saw the Middleton house across the street. I felt sick as I realized that my one time friend was now a threat to my career and my ability to provide for my family.

Upon entering the house I greeted the kids as though nothing was wrong. Ziggy came running and jumped in my lap. As I prepared dinner, I kept watching the clock anxious for LaVonna to come home. When she arrived, I greeted her with a smile and a kiss, but I was sure she knew something was wrong.

Later that evening, after the kids had gone to bed, we finally had a chance to talk. I could see the pain on LaVonna's face as I told her the story. Until now, I had been able to provide us with a beautiful home and opportunities I had only dreamed about as a child. Now, our financial security was at risk.

"Dennis, you've already done more than should be expected of anyone, maybe now is the time to think more about yourself," LaVonna gently offered.

"I know sweetheart, I just need to be sure that I'm

doing the right thing for the right reason." We talked until almost midnight. We prayed for peace, comfort, understanding and direction.

I awoke before sunrise and cuddled up next to LaVonna. She turned around and looked at me. "I can't do it sweetheart, it's about my integrity. I just can't do it," I whispered.

"I know, I've always known, everything is going to be ok," she replied.

I decided not to leave for work until 9:00 a.m., the official deadline for me to give Security the name. I sat in our bedroom listening to gospel music. The song that played, as I prepared to leave, was a spiritual that gave me encouragement and hope. I straightened my tie and adjusted my suit coat.

I chose to dress in a suit and tie for a couple reasons. First, as the old saying goes, "look good, feel good." Second, I hoped to plant the seed in Benson's mind that I was preparing to speak to the media. This might create just enough fear in his mind not to fire me today. I left the house knowing that I was doing the right thing and that I had LaVonna's love and support.

As I entered the building, I greeted my friend Blaine, the security guard. I rode the escalator to the second floor and walked to Benson's office. He was standing by his computer. I stood in the doorway.

"I just got to work," I announced.

"Did you give the name to Security?" he asked.

81

"No I did not…when will I know my punishment?" I asked.

Glaring, Benson answered, "By the end of the day."

"You need to make sure Grossenbacher is made aware of your decision. The outcome could cause harm to the company and result in public embarrassment," I told Benson.

As I said this, I was already contemplating going to the press if I were to be terminated. In my pocket I had the phone numbers of local TV reporters as well as the local newspaper.

"I'll be in and out of the office today, but I'll be back to find out my punishment," I told Benson as I left his office.

Chapter 25 –   A God Wink

I went to my office and called LaVonna. I told her that what Benson had said and that I was going to try to meet with our pastor, Bob Sherwood and then try to meet with my attorney, DeAnne Casperson. I called Bob's office and told the receptionist that it was extremely important that I meet with him. I was relieved when she said he could meet with me at 1:00 p.m. I then called DeAnne and told her what was going on. She told me to stop by her office after meeting with Bob.

At 10:25 a.m. I heard the beep of my computer letting me know that I had just received an email. I looked up at the monitor. The email was from Richard Cohen,

the investigator from the DOE Office of Hearings and
Appeals. I stared at the computer screen wondering what
was in the report. My stomach churned. If the report
found in BEA's favor it would likely embolden them
enough to terminate me by the end of the day. On the
other hand, if the report found in my favor there was the
likelihood that I would remain employed and even possibly
remain in my job.

My heart pounded as I read the several page
document. When I got to the end I just sat there. I had
neither won nor lost.

The report concluded that the case would proceed
to a formal hearing, and be decided by a hearing officer. I
breathed a sigh of relief. I knew that the prospect of a
hearing, and possibly losing, would make BEA think twice
about terminating me today.

I arrived at the church office promptly at 1:00,
"Hello Carolyn," I said to the office administrator.
Hearing my voice, Bob came out to greet me. Bob was the
new pastor and I didn't know him very well, but what I did
know I really liked. He seemed to have a real heart to
serve and a genuine compassion for people. As we sat
down at the table I tried to put on a brave front. I began
by telling him the events that had unfolded over the past
two years. I then described the stress of the past 24
hours.

"Pastor, I believe I made the right choice, but I
don't want to lose my job, I need to be able to take care of
my family. I don't understand why this is happening to
me." By this time, tears were rolling down my face. When
I looked up, I could see Bob's eyes moisten as well. I was

surprised to see such concern from someone who I barely knew.

"Dennis, God loves you, your faith will help you get through this. I believe you made the right and just decision. If they fire you, I'm sure there are many companies that would love to hire someone like you."

At the end of our conversation Bob prayed for me. His words comforted me beyond my expectations. We parted with a big hug.

Bolstered by my visit with Bob I drove across the river to DeAnne's office. We met for about an hour. She assessed my legal standing and the strength of my case. "Dennis, it is unlikely they will terminate you today, but you can never tell," she remarked at the end of our meeting.

I arrived back to work around 4:00 p.m. When I turned on my computer, I saw that Benson had sent me an email at 3:45. I opened the email. BEA had decided to postpone making a decision. I still had a job, for now. I felt numb, kind of like a death row inmate must feel when he receives a stay of execution. I was glad I had a chance for another day, but the guillotine continued to hang over my head.

Chapter 26 – Legal vs. Legal

Three days later on April 27, 2007 I called the DOE Hearing Officer, Valerie Adeyeye. I told her about BEA directing me to disclose a confidential source, and my refusal to do so. I expressed my fear that I could be terminated at any time.

"Please schedule the hearing as soon as possible,"
I pleaded.

Adeyeye said she would contact BEA and try to
schedule the hearing for early June. I was thrilled at the
prospect of having my day in court so soon. Until now, I
had consulted with DeAnne Casperson but I didn't intend
to have her represent me for the hearing. I felt fully
confident in my ability to represent myself and I knew it
would cost a lot of money.

I informed Adeyeye that I planned to represent
myself at the hearing. "That's totally acceptable but I
strongly suggest you consider obtaining an attorney,
especially for the hearing," she remarked.

That evening LaVonna and I discussed the phone
call with Adeyeye. LaVonna remarked, "I think it would
be wise to take the advice of Adeyeye."

I tried to convince LaVonna that with my
knowledge and experience of the whistleblower process I
could adequately represent myself. I also explained that
retaining an attorney would costs tens of thousands of
dollars that we didn't have.

Well, I lost that argument. The next day we met
with DeAnne. Because she knew me, the history of my
situation and had provided advice since June 2006, she
agreed to take my case. However, she was concerned
because she had no prior experience with the DOE 708
whistleblower process. I told her it didn't matter because I
had extensive experience including being a witness for the
laboratory in a previous case.

DeAnne estimated it would cost at least $30,000

DENNIS PATTERSON

dollars for her to represent me. LaVonna and I looked at each other as our jaws dropped. We knew that if we prevailed BEA would have to pay the costs but if we lost this would create an incredible hardship on us. By the time we left her office, there was no doubt that we needed her on our team, no matter the cost.

On May 10, after coming home from a long and stressful day, I picked up the mail and noticed a letter with a return address from Seattle Washington, "Halvorson Saunders & Willner, PLLC." The letter was my notification that this law firm would be representing BEA, in association with BEA legal staff. It surprised me that BEA would be willing to spend what could be upwards of hundreds of thousands of dollars to defend a DOE whistleblower case.

Under DOE Code of Federal Regulations 708, BEA was at little to no financial risk. Whistleblowers are not able to gain financially. The only monies available to a DOE whistleblower are those that are taken from them such as loss of job, loss of merit increase, suspension and attorney costs. I had never heard of a DOE contractor retaining outside legal representation for a whistleblower case, and certainly never at the INL.

Chapter 27 – Third Investigation

It was a beautiful, warm day in May when I received a phone call from Ms. Toni Vandel, BEA Employee Relations and Diversity Specialist. She told me that she needed to speak to me the following day. When I asked her why we were meeting she said she was tasked by management to conduct an investigation. Later that day, I

learned via email that I was being investigated for
"behavior and/or actions in the meeting held on April 24
with Benson and Middleton. "

The following day I sat at my desk and prayed as I
prepared to walk downstairs and meet with Vandel. When
I arrived, I discovered that the interrogation was being
conducted by Vandel's manager, Arantza Zabala. We sat
at the round table with Zabala nearest me, asking the
questions and Vandel on the far side of the table taking
notes. I knew both of them very well, having worked with
them for many years. In fact, Zabala and I had conducted
interviews together in the past.

Zabala began, "Doug Benson and Tom Middleton
have asked us to investigate you. They allege that you did
not treat them with dignity and respect in the April 24
meeting."

I took a deep breath and said, "I don't think it was
fair for them to put me in that situation. I was intimidated
and harassed to disclose a confidential source and now I'm
the one being investigated…this is wrong."

Zabala cited several statements that I allegedly
made that demonstrated I hadn't treated Benson and
Middleton respectfully. As she read each one I replied
with "ok" acknowledging that I understood what she was
saying. There was only one statement that I admitted was
less than professional. This was when I remarked, "Tom
you are doing a great job as Security director." I felt as
though it really didn't matter what I said or didn't say to
Vandel and Zabala.

It was clear to me that BEA wasn't interested in
the truth. They were intent on continuing the pattern of

intimidation, abuse and retaliation. Since I filed the whistle blower complaint on June 1, 2006, this was the third time I had been investigated for alleged misconduct.

Chapter 28 – We'll Never Know

Three more weeks passed and I still hadn't been told what disciplinary action would be taken against me. I continued to perform my job the best that I could, but there wasn't much to do. Over the past several months very few employees had contacted the office for assistance. I spent most of my time reading procedures and evaluating my own situation.

On June 9, I received an anonymous letter that contained a very serious allegation. The letter alleged that BEA had been promoting and unfairly compensating an employee who was a close relative of a national politician. Supposedly, this was being done to gain favor with the politician and thereby improve INL's posture in Washington D.C.

This was not the first time the INL had received an allegation like this. In the late 90's I had investigated a similar complaint and found no merit to the allegation. Nonetheless, I believed we had an obligation to at least review the current complaint. Later that afternoon I gave the letter to Benson, who in turn notified Middleton.

Middleton responded via email noting that because a similar issue had been addressed previously no further action was warranted. Middleton expressed his displeasure that we would even consider investigating this anonymous complaint. To Benson's credit, he wrote back to Middleton and told him that a meeting should be

convened as soon as possible so that we could agree upon
a path forward.

Benson tasked me with scheduling a meeting with
Security, Legal, Human Resources, and myself. I
scheduled the meeting for the afternoon of June 14, 2007.
Little did I know that this would be the last I would ever
hear or know anything about this issue.

Chapter 29 – The Verdict

On June 13, 2007 Benson stopped in the doorway
of my office, "come to my office now," he said. When I
arrived Zabala was seated at the table. Benson told me to
take a seat. I knew this was the moment. I had a terrible
sick feeling in my stomach. My heart was racing and my
palms sweating. This time I didn't have the chance to pray
prior to the meeting. I remained silent. My years of
experience told me that a final decision had been made and
no matter what I said things were not going to change. I
decided to just listen and accept whatever I was told. I
looked at Benson and Zabala. Benson glared at me, as he
peered over his reading glasses. Zabala pushed her hair
back from her face and leaned forward with an
exaggerated sense of authority.

I sat across from Zabala and diagonally from
Benson. I took a deep breath. I noticed a letter in
Benson's hand. He placed it on the table and pushed it
toward me.

"Management has decided to remove you from

the Employee Concerns/Ethics Office," Benson said.

"One of the reasons is your failure to treat Tom and me with respect and as you see on page two your failure to disclose the name of the confidential employee."

I sat there silently and listened. Although I was hurting and angry, I chose not to argue or defend myself. I knew that it would do no good, and that anything I might say could be used against me.

Benson continued, "Your removal is effective immediately, let's go to your office. You can pack up your personal stuff and I'll take you over to meet your new manager."

When we got to my office, Zabala stood in the doorway and Benson sat down. They watched as I removed pictures from the wall and gathered personal items such as birthday cards, cups, and awards. I paused as I picked up the family photo on my desk. I felt numb, as I pondered how I would explain to Jasmine and Darius why I was no longer the Ethics Officer.

Benson interrupted my thought, "Dennis, let's go. I'll introduce you to your new manager."

"No thank you," I said. "I'm going home. I can meet him tomorrow." Benson seemed annoyed, but he didn't challenge me.

I caught the escalator down to the lobby. As I walked past the Security desk, I remembered taking this same path when I was suspended for three days in October, 2006. But this time, when I return, I will no longer be the INL Ethics Officer/Employee Concerns manager.

I sat in the parking lot. My body shook and my

head ached. I don't remember what I was thinking, I just
felt a deep sense of loss and despair. I decided not to call
LaVonna. I wanted to tell her in person.

It was a sunny day, so I drove along the river on
my way home. Many times before, I had driven by the
river as a way of unwinding and calming my spirit. I tried
to grasp the gravity of what had just happened and what
life would look like in the future.

By the time I arrived home, I was composed and
able to greet Darius and Jasmine like I always do. When
LaVonna came home, I motioned towards the bedroom
and said we needed to talk. I took her in my arms,
"Sweetheart, I'm no longer the Ethics Officer. Benson
removed me today…it hurts so much."

"I can't believe they did this to you, this is so
wrong," she cried.

"I know, I feel like going across the street and
banging on Tom's door. I feel like going to Benson's
house and punching him in the face. This is so damn
unfair!"

"Its ok babe, everything's going to be ok. I love
you and the kids love you," she responded.

We sat on the bed for several minutes with our
arms around each other. We then decided it was time to
tell the Darius and Jasmine.

We walked into the family room. They were
seated on the couch watching TV. LaVonna and I sat
across from them on the loveseat. I turned off the TV.

"Hey kids, I need to talk to you for a minute, you know how much I love my job." I paused, "Well, as of today I am no longer the Ethics Officer." Their faces went blank.

"Why dad, what happened?"

"Well, as I've taught you, keeping your word is one of the most important things you can do. In my case, I kept a promise to an employee who asked me not to tell anyone his or her name. Doug Benson and Tom Middleton tried to make me disclose the name. When I refused, Doug removed me from my job. Some of these things have been going on for more than a year, but I didn't tell you because I didn't want you to be worried. I love you guys so much."

"We love you too dad," they said as we joined in a big family hug. I knew at this moment that whatever the future, I would always have my faith, family and friends and that was what was most important.

Chapter 30 – Integrity

The next morning, I was mentally and emotionally prepared to return to work and meet my new boss. I was anxious to find out what my new job duties would be and to begin building a good relationship with my new management team.

I stopped by Benson's office. As it turned out, my new manager's office was just down the hall from my old office. Doug introduced me to my new boss, Ed Anderson and left without any explanation. Also present was Ed's boss, Deb Tate. Both looked very

uncomfortable, but they did their best to make me feel
comfortable. I shook their hands and told them I looked
forward to the new challenge.

Deb began, "Our organization is called
Engineering Services. Our mission is to provide
engineering services to organizations throughout the
INL." After several minutes of describing the
organization the discussion then turned to my job
description.

"Dennis, your title will be Management Systems
Process Lead. You will report directly to Ed and your role
will be to provide engineering support to engineers and
managers," Deb explained.

It was clear to me that I didn't have the
experience or education needed to be successful in this
role or organization.

"Ed, may I see the written job description for this
job," I asked. Ed opened up his folder and handed it to
me. Just as I suspected, the requirements read, "bachelor's
degree plus 15 years or advanced degree and 13 years of
extensive engineering experience, exposure and command
of engineering design, analysis and configuration
management process and principles."

"I have zero engineering experience and my
degree is in business," I told them.

Ed slumped in his chair and Deb dropped her pen
on the desk. It was as though I had told them I was from
another planet.

"What makes you think I am qualified for this job,

I asked,

"Well, you must be very good because you're currently in a senior level position," Deb stated.

"Yes, I am very good at what I do, but I am not an engineer and do not have the required qualifications," I responded.

Ed interjected, "Dennis, prior to this, we didn't have any knowledge about your experience or education, but I will commit to do whatever is necessary to give you a fair chance to succeed."

"And I will do my absolute best to make this work," I said.

Ed walked me over to my new office. It was a cubicle with a window that faced one of the equipment buildings. I had the feeling that this was a not so subtle message on the part of Benson and others. I had gone from a comfortable office with privacy to a cubicle where everyone could see and hear me.

A couple days later, Ed presented me with a new Position Description. The job duties were revised and the qualifications modified. I would now be holding review meetings with engineers and updating procedures. Not very challenging or rewarding, but at least it afforded me an opportunity to succeed. Ed had been true to his word.

On June 19, 2007 I learned that a long time and well respected senior manager, Dr. Jim Lake was retiring from BEA. Dr. Lake had been a senior manager for the past ten years. In addition, he had served a term as the President of the American Nuclear Society. Jim and I worked several issues together and we shared a mutual respect for each other. I suspected that his retirement was related to the fact that BEA had previously replaced him as

director of Nuclear Science & Technology. I was sorry he
was retiring. Jim was one of only three BEA senior
managers that knew my long history of contributions to
the success of the laboratory. Jim was a person with great
integrity.

I sent an email to Jim thanking him for his ethical
leadership. He responded as follows, "Thanks Dennis,
you've been wonderful to work with, and you've made it
easy for us managers to do the right thing." Receiving
such a message from someone of Dr. Lake's stature made
me feel good and proud.

The next day I sent an email to another senior
manager, Dr. Harold Blackman. Earlier Blackman had
invited me to be a member of the INL Institutional
Review Board. The Board was chartered with ensuring
that any INL research and/or experiments that involved
human subjects met the highest ethical standards and
protected the rights and dignity of the subjects. I was
honored by the request and had gladly accepted.

But now, I had a responsibility and obligation to
inform Blackman that I had been involuntarily removed
from the Ethics/Employee Concerns office. I anticipated
that with this knowledge, he might feel compelled to ask
me to resign as a member of the Board.

Instead, he wrote back and asked me to remain on
the Board. Harold was another BEA manager that
demonstrated integrity.

Once again, I felt a sense of pride. The dichotomy
created here was quite amazing. On the one hand I was
deemed to be so unethical that I had to be removed from
the Ethics Officer position, but on the other hand I was

representing the company on a Board that was tasked with ensuring research and experiments were conducted ethically.

On June 25, 2007 I attended Dr. Lake's retirement party. Senator Larry Craig's Idaho Falls regional director, Knut Meyerin read a letter that had been entered into the congressional record by Senator Craig. The letter acknowledged Dr. Lake for his great contributions to the laboratory and to nuclear energy. I had met Knut earlier in the year at Skyline High School. He and I were both members of the Skyline Character Education Coalition.

At the end of Lake's retirement party, I visited with Knut. He asked me how I was doing and about my job. I told him about my whistleblower case and the actions taken by management.

He responded, "You know Dennis it's not unusual for someone like you to report an issue and then be retaliated against. Please send more information about your situation."

I later sent him an email with a link to my whistleblower complaint that was on the DOE website. The next day I received an email from Knut, "Hi Dennis, yes, I did find it and downloaded the information. If you feel my presence at your hearing will help, let me know."

I was honored to know that a representative from the office of a United States Senator was willing to attend my hearing as a way of showing his support. I replied, "I think it would help and I would love for you to attend."

Chapter 31 – Public Disclosure

On June 27, two days after talking to Knut, I received a call, "Hi Dennis, my name is Paul Menser, a reporter with the Post Register. I have a copy of your complaint from the DOE website, my editor has asked me to write a story."

I responded, "How do you even know about this?"

"Well, my editor gave me the copy and asked me to do a story," he replied.

At this point I was not comfortable speaking to the press. I had heard too many stories about how information is often misrepresented by the media. With this thought in mind, I kept my answers brief. I focused on the misconduct that I reported and the retaliatory actions including the intimidation, low performance appraisal, and being removed from the Ethics Office.

The next morning, there it was on the front page of the Post Register, "INL Whistle-blower turns to DOE to get complaints heard." The story included the fact that I had uncovered problems in the Security organization and had filed a whistle blower complaint in June 2006. It further stated that DOE Idaho had dismissed my complaint, but that the DOE Office of Hearings and Appeals reinstated the complaint. Overall, the story was accurate and balanced.

One piece of the article caught my attention. It contained a quote from Steve Kohn, President of the

Washington D. C. based, National Whistleblowers Association. "Kohn said the administrative path Patterson is following was designed by DOE to keep its employees in the dark about the better remedy available from the Department of Labor. Number one you want independence...Whistleblowers cases can get politicized very fast, and DOE and DOE contract managers are very close when it comes to matters like this."

In my opinion, Mr. Kohn was absolutely correct. I had already experienced this when the DOE attorney weighed in on my 708 complaint back in July of 2006.

In many respects I was relieved and pleased that the information was now in the public domain. I believed that the more people that knew about my whistleblower complaint, the more BEA would be compelled to make positive changes to the work place.

Chapter 32 – Mediation

The Hearing Officer, Valerie Adeyeye, had rescheduled the whistleblower hearing to begin August 21, 2007. However, she encouraged both sides to consider using mediation, with the possibility of avoiding a trial. Of course, BEA quickly jumped at the opportunity. I didn't like the idea because mediation would only address issues such as my lost merit, job title, and suspension without pay. For me, the more important issue was getting my day in court so that the truth would be known. This would likely compel BEA to make fundamental changes to the work environment such that INL employees would not be punished for raising issues and they would feel valued and respected.

After discussing this with LaVonna, and
consulting with DeAnne, I decided to participate in the
mediation with BEA.

We quickly learned that although BEA wanted to
mediate, they certainly didn't want to mediate in good
faith. BEA conditioned the offer to mediate by stating
unequivocally that they would not even consider
reinstating me as the Ethics Officer/Employee Concerns
manager.

The morning of the mediation session, I arrived at
DeAnne's office at 9:00 a.m. She directed me to the
conference room. I had spent many hours in this room
over the past several months. It was a large room with a
great view of the Snake River. She left me there and said
she would return when the BEA team arrived.

BEA was late. The clock ticked slowly, finally the
door opened and DeAnne walked in with the two BEA
representatives. The first was Arantza Zabala, the same
person who had investigated me in May. The second was
BEA senior attorney, Katherine Moriarty, the person who
had requested the investigation of me in June of 2006. I
found it odd that BEA selected two individuals that were
part of the retaliation to represent the interests of the INL.

The mediator was an older fellow. He slowly
shuffled to his chair on the other side of the conference
table. He was clearly one who had enjoyed too many good
meals. He struggled a bit to get comfortable in the chair.
He opened his brief case and flipped through a large stack
of documents. I observed him carefully in order to get a
sense of who he was and how he might conduct the
session. He reminded me of an old country lawyer. He

had the mannerism and style of TV's Matlock. He began by explaining the mediation process and the expectations.

The morning and first part of the afternoon was spent with everyone in the same room discussing facts, disagreeing at times, and positioning for the latter part of the mediation. During the discussion of one my alleged acts of misconduct the mediator said, "This is really trivial and blown way out of proportion."

By late afternoon he had the opposing sides go to separate rooms. He explained that he would be shuttling between the two rooms in an effort to come to an agreement.

During the next several hours, several offers and counter offers were sent across the two rooms. As the clock approached 9:00 p.m. the sun was beginning to set and I was exhausted. We had been at this nonstop for almost twelve hours.

It appeared as though we might reach a resolution. As we got closer to agreement, I began to feel nauseous. I felt like I might throw up. I realized that if we were to reach a settlement agreement, the past two years were for nothing more than getting back what had been taken away.

BEA was not willing to acknowledge wrong doing, they were simply trying to make the issues go away. There would be no changes in the work environment and no one would know what really happened.

Finally, around eleven o'clock DeAnne made our final offer. Zabala and Moriarty said they didn't have the authority to sign off on it. They said that they would present the offer to BEA senior management, but they would not recommend approval.

Frustrated, and exhausted I left the building and

drove home.

LaVonna and the kids met me at the door. Before I said a word, they knew from my face that the fight wasn't over. Slowly, I began telling them what it was like to spend the entire day and most of the night trying to resolve things. I told them how hard it was to have to tell the story and relive all of the feelings and emotions. It was well past midnight before we all went to bed. After a long hard day it was so good to have the love and support of my family.

The next day BEA made a counter offer that was totally unacceptable. I respectfully declined.

I told DeAnne to contact BEA and extend my best and final offer. I would agree to a resolution if BEA would: 1) pay attorney fees, 2) remove all discipline from my file and reimburse me for the three days off without pay, 3) assign me to a new job comparable to my previous position and 4) award me a 4% retroactive merit pay increase.

Almost immediately I regretted making the offer for the same reasons as before. Settling would not result in any changes in the work environment and the only person helped was me. In addition, I didn't trust that Zabala and Moriarty would find a suitable position for me. The last time they found me a job I got stuck being a make-believe engineer.

That evening I discussed my reservations with LaVonna. She fully understood my concerns but we agreed that I was obligated to honor the offer if BEA accepted.

The next day my phone rang. DeAnne called to inform me that Moriarty said all conditions of my offer would be met with one exception. Moriarty said they would only give me a 3% raise instead of 4% because, "Dennis needed to accept more responsibility."

I was dumbfounded. The dollar difference between 3% and 4% was only $25/week. Why on earth would BEA risk hundreds of thousands of dollars, the cost of going to trial, when they could reach a settlement for almost nothing? Whatever the reason, I was relieved.

I told DeAnne to tell BEA I was declining the offer and that I wanted the DOE hearing to proceed. DeAnne expressed surprise that I would decline the counter offer over $25 a week. But, she said she respected my decision and would convey the message to BEA.

The following morning, DeAnne called me again. She sounded troubled and distressed, "Dennis I just got a call from the Mediator, we need to talk. I need you to come down to my office."

"Sure, I'll be right down," I responded. I knew something was very wrong. I turned off my computer and headed downtown.

When I entered her office we sat down at the large wooden table. The look on her face told me this was not good.

She began, "Dennis, the call from the mediator was something I've never experienced before. I may be wrong, but the mediator seemed to be pressuring me to get you to settle. He said that in his opinion if we were to lose you might pursue legal action against me."

My jaw clenched and my hands trembled. It felt like everything was falling apart. If my attorney was

having doubts, how could I win my case? Had BEA
contacted the Mediator and influenced him to intimidate
my attorney?

I closed my eyes for a moment, took a deep
breath and said, "DeAnne, this isn't just about me, it's
about wanting to make things better...I don't want anyone
to have to go through what I have gone through."

My voice quivered as I attempted to get her to
understand. Finally, she said, "Dennis, I get it. I'm with
you. Thank you for coming down and talking to me."

A few weeks later I was in DeAnne's office
preparing for the trial when she received a phone call from
BEA General Counsel, Mark Olsen. His message: "If it
is just a matter of money we can resolve this without
having a hearing."

I responded, "DeAnne, tell Olsen it was never
about money. I want my day in court."

A couple weeks later the Hearing Officer
scheduled the Hearing to convene on Tuesday, November
27. She estimated the trial would take four days.

Chapter 33 – Politics

With all of the challenges and obstacles at work I
decided it was a good time to pursue other ways to
contribute to the lives of others. For the past several years
I had considered running for public office. The more I

read in the papers the more I became convinced that now was the time. The Idaho Falls City Council had experienced some rather embarrassing episodes. In fact, one of the council members had disclosed allegations of misconduct on the part of a couple of city division directors.

LaVonna and I had several heart to heart discussions about my running for a Council seat. She expressed several reservations about my running. Her biggest concern was the impact to our family life at a time when we needed each other the most.

Eventually, we agreed that this would be a positive thing for us and for the community. We believed that it was time for a change in Idaho Falls, just as it was time for a change in our country.

On August 12, 2007, I officially declared my candidacy for a seat on the Idaho Falls City Council. As a lifelong and dedicated democrat I knew that running for a partisan position such as state legislature was pretty much a losing proposition. However, the city council seats were non-partisan and hence I figured I had a shot at winning. I entered the race having no prior political experience, but confident that my experience, education and reputation would make me a viable candidate. My biggest worry was that my pending whistleblower complaint could work against me.

LaVonna agreed to be my treasurer. We spent long hours before and after work and on weekends going door to door and talking with people. My greatest pleasure from campaigning was the opportunity to listen to the concerns of others. On occasion, I would meet someone who knew my parents or one of my siblings. Without fail, they would tell me good things about my family.

One of the unique experiences was "Live Wire" hosted by the Post Register. Each candidate went down to the newspaper, logged onto the internet and provided members of the community an opportunity to ask questions and make comments. I was asked which of the presidential candidates I most admired and whose ideas aligned with mine. I paused, and thought about not answering the question. I knew that if I answered truthfully it could damage my chances, but…I typed, "Barack Obama."

With the campaign well underway, I awoke early each morning and read the paper to keep abreast of local happenings. The morning of October 7, 2007, it was reported that Idaho Senator Larry Craig had just been elected to the Idaho Hall of Fame.

Earlier in the year, Craig had been arrested in a Minneapolis airport bathroom. He had been cited for improper conduct by soliciting an encounter with an undercover male police officer. Given this incident, and the fact that Craig failed to disclose his arrest, I was dismayed that he had been elected. Across the nation, Craig was the butt of jokes and the subject of ridicule on talk shows. In my opinion, this was an embarrassment to our state.

According the article, John Grossenbacher had also been elected to the Idaho Hall of Fame. I was dismayed by this as well, but for different reasons. Grossenbacher had only lived in Idaho about two and half years and from my knowledge his sole Idaho contribution was being president of the INL. The legacy of the INL and Grossenbacher's contribution were yet to be determined.

The month of October was a good month. I was busy with campaigning and my day to day work life was going pretty well. I was getting quite skilled at pretending to be an engineer.

As the end of the month approached I was looking forward to the conclusion of the campaign, but there was still a lot of work to do. Most mornings LaVonna and I would get up early and walk through neighborhoods handing out brochures.

Chapter 34 – Fourth Investigation

On October 23, LaVonna and I had completed our scheduled campaign route and left for work. The day was pretty much like any other, but as the lunch hour approached, I received a call from Toni Vandel.

"You need to come to Arantza's office, Torrance has lodged a complaint against you," she said.

"What am I accused of this time, I replied.

"You'll find out when you get here," was all she would say.

Over the next couple of hours, I pondered what Torrance could be complaining about. The last time I saw him was approximately a month ago. We had exited the men's room near Vandel's office. Torrance was ahead of me as we walked towards the main lobby. As we approached the escalator, I decided to ask Torrance a question. I wanted to know if, and how long, they kept the tape recordings of Security interviews.

I walked behind him for a short distance, waiting for an opportune time to speak to him. As he entered the cubicle area, just north of the escalator, he stopped to talk to a colleague. Seeing that he was occupied, I decided not to ask him the question. I turned around and went back to my office. It was unfathomable that this incident could be the source of my being investigated again.

When I entered Zabala's office, I was offered a seat.

Zabala began, "Torrance has formally charged you with following him with the intent to intimidate him." This time was I livid. In less than 18 months, I was being investigated for the fourth time.

"Did you follow Torrance about a month ago," Zabala asked.

"Yes, but only to ask him a question," I replied.

"Torrance has alleged that you intended to intimidate him," she said.

I could tell by the tone of her voice and her mannerisms that she believed Torrance and discounted what I was saying.

I looked across the table at Zabala and Vandel. They both appeared to be enjoying the moment. My admission that I had followed Torrance seemed to please them, as though I had just admitted to some egregious act of misconduct.

"This is totally unfair, it's wrong to interrogate me again because of a simple misunderstanding," I said loudly.

"Not only that, but you guys screwed up when you didn't tell Ed Anderson that I had zero engineering experience. Next time, be honest with the manager. You can investigate me all you want, once a month, once a week or every day, it doesn't matter. I haven't done anything wrong," I said as I left Zabala's office.

Chapter 35 – The Vote

On November 4th my picture along with three other city council candidates was on the front page of the Post Register. It provided each of us an opportunity to answer common questions. My answers reflected my commitment to being a voice for everyone. I spoke about the need to consider all issues with the guiding principles of fairness, honesty, integrity and compassion. After a long campaign the election was just two days away. Jasmine and Darius, along with other family and friends, had helped with the campaign. Everyone had been encouraging and supportive.

With Election Day upon us, LaVonna and I were hopeful. On the night of the election we invited supporters to our home to watch the returns come in and celebrate with us. Unfortunately, things didn't go as planned. As the returns started coming in, it was clear that this wasn't going to be a good night for me. Everyone expressed words of encouragement as they left. Most didn't wait for the final vote count. I smiled and thanked them, but the hurt was deeper than I had expected.

A few days after the election one of the city
council members announced he had been called to go on
an LDS mission and was resigning his seat on the council.
According to the newspaper the mayor indicated he would
be selecting the interim replacement within the next few
weeks. The mayor was quoted as saying he wanted to
name someone who would contribute to making the city
council more, "well rounded."

Several friends told me they had contacted the
mayor and recommended that he select me as the interim
city councilman. LaVonna and I discussed whether it
made sense for me to speak to the mayor. I was
apprehensive to put my name in consideration because I
didn't want to experience disappointment so soon after the
election.

On November 11, 2007 I met with Mayor
Fuhriman. I made my case that I was the right person at
the right time to help lead the city. I emphasized my
experience as the Ethics Officer for the laboratory. I
explained how I could contribute to the decision making
of the city leadership and emphasized the importance of
ethics and transparency in government.

The Mayor was polite and courteous in his
response, but it appeared that he had already made up his
mind. He graciously shook my hand and said he would
add my name to the list. I thanked him for his time and
wished him well.

A few weeks later, it was announced that the
Mayor selected a highly qualified and competent
replacement, whether or not this person made the council
more "well rounded," only time would tell.

Chapter 36 – How Black is Black?

On November 12, I was deposed by BEA's outside counsel, Larry Halvorson. As DeAnne and I entered the INL law library a white haired gentleman rose to greet us. He introduced himself and took a seat opposite of where we sat down.

Over the next few hours, Halverson grilled me with questions. He asked about everything from where I lived to conversations going back two years. I was a bit troubled by a particular exchange. Halvorson was apparently trying to discredit my allegation that racial discrimination was a factor in the revocation of Loren's site access. The following exchange occurred:

> Halvorson, "Had, in fact Jodi indicated to you that she knew Loren was African American before she pulled his access?"

> Patterson, "No, She indicated she pulled his picture up before pulling it."

> "Halvorson, "Okay, and his picture would indicate that he was African American, correct?"

> Patterson, "Yes"

> Halvorson, "He's black, I take it?"

> Patterson, "I'm not following your question."

> Halvorson, "His skin color is black?"

> Patterson, "No"

> Halvorson, "Oh, it's not?"

Patterson, "No"

Halvorson, "Loren isn't?"

Patterson, "No"

Halvorson, "Is he darker than you or lighter than you?"

Patterson, "Darker but not black."

Halvorson, "Okay, but you think that by looking at his picture, that she would have known that he was African American?"

Patterson: "Yes"

Halvorson: "I haven't seen his picture so I don't know."

Patterson: "When you said black, I presumed you meant color, and he's not black. He's African American."

Halverson: "His skin color is dark; is that correct?"

Patterson: "Yes"

I found this questioning to be quite disturbing. It seemed to me that Halverson believed that an African American must have black skin or at the very least very dark skin.

Chapter 37 – Round One

In October 2007 BEA had filed a summary judgment with the Hearing Officer, Adeyeye. The summary judgment was filed with the intent of getting my original retaliation complaint (filed June 2006) dismissed. Because we hadn't heard anything by now, DeAnne and I presumed that the Hearing Officer wasn't going to grant the judgment.

On November 21, a week before the hearing we received an official response from Adeyeye. Adeyeye ruled largely in favor of BEA. Adeyeye dismissed five of the six allegations cited in my original whistle blower complaint. My biggest disappointment was that Adeyeye had made her decision without the benefit of testimony.

For two days, I mulled over the Summary Judgment. Finally, I realized that while I disagreed with Adeyeye's conclusions, they were consistent with DOE regulations. I was comforted by the fact that her decision was based on DOE administrative requirements, not on the merits of my complaint.

DeAnne and I decided not to appeal. We believed that the retaliatory actions that BEA took after I filed my whistleblower complaint were of greater significance and would be easier to prove. These actions included, investigating me four times, disciplining me with time off without pay, and removing me from the Ethics Officer/Employee Concerns position.

LaVonna and I spent the weekend with family and friends. I spent most of Monday in DeAnne's office going over facts, dates, times, places, and people. The case file was well over a thousand pages with numerous citations and notations. The process would have been overwhelming except for the fact that I had lived and breathed the information over the past three years. I had the benefit of knowing the information and the knowledge that the truth didn't change with circumstance or time.

Chapter 38 – The Hearing, Day One

The DOE hearing began on Tuesday, November 27, 2007. I awoke with a sense of excitement. My day in court had finally arrived. As usual, I went outside to get the newspaper. The front page headline read, "DOE Hearing Starts Today." I prepared my papers, put on my suit and tie and was ready to go. LaVonna, Jasmine and Darius were ready and waiting.

I had expected the hearing to be in one of the large courtrooms. When I opened the door, my jaw dropped. It was a small make shift room with a table up front for the Hearing Officer and uncomfortable looking chairs for the attorneys, witnesses and observers. As I approached the front of the room, I did a double take when I saw an African American female. We greeted each other as she was leaving the room. It was only after she had passed, that I realized that she had introduced herself as, "Valerie Adeyeye." It hit me, she was the Hearing Officer.

Growing up in Idaho Falls, I had never seen an African American judge, hearing officer or any other official of the judicial system. It felt good knowing that the case would be decided by an African American. DeAnne and I had speculated that BEA might try the "angry black man" strategy in an effort to portray me in a negative light. If it was part of their strategy, I was sure they now had second thoughts. When Katherine

Moriarity (BEA attorney) and Halvorson saw Adeyeye, they almost tripped over each other.

Adeyeye opened the hearing with a description of the DOE hearing process and what to expect over the next four days. I was pleased to see reporters from local television stations & the Post Register. Also present, was an investigator from the DOE Inspector General's Office.

When one of the TV reporters prepared to set up her video camera, Adeyeye interrupted, "Cameras will not be allowed in the courtroom."

Adeyeye then asked everyone present to introduce themselves. Members of my family included my sisters Norma Patterson, Judy Patterson, and Lou Swift; nephew Lee Swift (Angie); niece Nicole Swift with her daughters Keisha & Mia, and my brother Don Patterson. My pastor, Bob Sherwood also attended.

Upon seeing that I had so many family members present, Adeyeye commented, "You could have an early Thanksgiving right here."

DeAnne presented her opening statement, "Essentially the case we have today deals with Mr. Patterson and the actions that he has taken to protect his own standards, his integrity, and the standards of BEA. I want to begin by giving you a quote from his most recent Performance Evaluation. This occurred in February 24th of 2006. Doug Benson, his immediate Manager, in referring to Mr. Patterson, said: 'He knows and lives the standards without compromise.' And Mr. Benson is right. Mr. Patterson is willing to sacrifice his position, his chance of success, even his employment to protect BEA standards. But when he did so, he was subjected to retaliation. What he was not willing to sacrifice is his integrity, his personal standards, and BEA standards in the risks that their management caused."

Halvorson followed with his opening
argument. I listened to him state that I had misused
government equipment, failed to cooperate with Security's
investigations and that I was insubordinate by failing to
disclose the confidential name.

At times, I could feel my blood pressure rise and my pulse
quicken. It was hard to suppress the urge to interrupt
when he said something that was untrue.

Following Halverson's remarks, DeAnne
called me to the stand and I was sworn in. DeAnne and I
had previously agreed that it would be best if I was the
first person to testify. We believed it would be important
for me to establish credibility with the hearing officer as
soon as possible.

I took the witness chair, just a few feet from
LaVonna and the kids. DeAnne had me review my
personal history as well as my professional history at the
laboratory. She had me read aloud excerpts from the past
few year's performance appraisals. With pride and
humility I read the words that spoke about my outstanding
performance, and my commitment to setting the highest
standards in ethical conduct.

DeAnne spent the rest of the day going over the
facts and having me testify as to my actions and the
actions of BEA management. By the end of the day, I was
tired but feeling good. Day one had been a good day. We
had established the foundation for proving that BEA had
indeed retaliated against me for filing the whistleblower
complaint.

As we walked out of the hearing room, one of the waiting television reporters asked about the hearing.

"I believe that we are off to a great start…justice will be served," I said.

That evening my family gathered around the dinner table and gave thanks. The Swifts visited for a couple of hours before driving back to Boise. We encouraged them to spend the night because it was beginning to snow and the roads would likely be dangerous. Unfortunately, they had to return to work the next morning. By the time they left it was close to ten o'clock. As I prepared for bed, I thanked LaVonna and the kids for all their love and support. I knew that tomorrow would be the most challenging day for me. DeAnne had warned me that Halverson's cross-examination would be grueling.

Chapter 39 – Hearing, Day 2

The next morning, as I prepared to leave, the phone rang. It was my sister Lou. She sounded exhausted. I asked her about the trip back to Boise.

She paused, then said, "Well, you know Buzz, we are lucky just to be alive. We were about halfway home when we slid off the road, the SUV was on two wheels."

"Oh my goodness," I exclaimed.

"If not for the grace of God we wouldn't be here," she replied.

Grateful that they were ok, I said, "I love you

Lou."

When LaVonna and I arrived at the courthouse,
we were pleased to see my sister Norma already there and
waiting for us. We gave her a hug and walked into the
room. A few minutes later Adeyeye arrived and I was
sworn in. Halvorson began his cross examination.

Halverson spoke in a soft and deliberate manner.
His presence was more comfortable than I expected.

He opened, "Do you believe you could effectively
return to the position of Employee Concerns Manager?"

I replied, "Yes, but only if Grossenbacher created
the right work environment. He would have to set the
standard by allowing employees to express their opinions."

Halvorson then attempted to make the case that
BEA had an "open door policy" and that I had always had
free access to speak to Grossenbacher. I told Halvorson
that BEA had no such policy and reminded him that back
in 2005, when I told Olsen I intended to meet with
Grossenbacher, he responded with, "Do you really want to
take me on?"

Halvorson spent considerable time cross
examining me on my actions and statements on April 24,
2007. It was the meeting in which I refused to disclose the
name of the confidential employee. He asked several
times whether in the past I had spoken to and challenged
Benson as I had in this meeting. I shared previous
examples where Benson and I had passionate discussions
and strong disagreements. I told Halvorson I acted

ethically and responsibly by honoring the request of the employee that I not disclose the name to anyone.

"It was wrong for Benson and Middleton to try to force me to give up the name. For me to do so would be in violation of the INL Standards of Conduct and Business Ethics," I said.

I also explained that I had consulted with Dan Robertson, Employee Concerns Program Manager for ICP, and that Dan agreed that I should not disclose the name.

Halvorson questioned me about the August 2005 meeting with Juan Alvarez. Halvorson attempted to portray my conduct as inappropriate and unprofessional.

"All I did was express an opinion that he didn't want to hear," I responded.

I noted that I informed Alvarez that his security managers had violated procedures and refused to cooperate with my investigation. I further testified, "I told Alvarez that I believed racial discrimination was a factor and if Loren had filed a complaint with the Idaho Human Rights Commission (IHRC) BEA would have lost." I reminded Halvorson that Alvarez issued a letter the very next day that basically described me as being unfit to be the Employee Concerns/Ethics Officer.

Halvorson then moved to the issue of whether I had violated company policy by writing and filing my whistleblower complaint on company time and equipment.

"This should never have been a question. A DOE contractor employee indisputably has the right to file a DOE whistle blower complaint, and do so on company equipment and time," I said.

The questioning then turned to the cell phone
conversation I had with Security investigator, Torrance. In
September 2006, Torrance had called me while I was at the
hospital with my friend AJ. This was the conversation
where according to Torrance, I refused to cooperate with
him. I explained that when Torrance asked me if anyone
had told me why I was being investigated I told him I was
choosing to not answer at that time. I told Halvorson I
was well within my rights to not answer that question and
that it was unfair for BEA to later discipline me for this.

"AJ died the next day," I told Halvorson.

On redirect examination, DeAnne asked me about
the Battelle Memorial Corporate investigative report dated
December 2005. She read an excerpt from the report, "We
recommend that BEA senior management evaluate and
identify actions it considers appropriate to improve the
working relationships between the Ethics Office and the
involved managers and departments in this matter."

"Did BEA take any actions in response to this
recommendation," she asked.

"No, they did nothing, if they had perhaps things
might have turned out differently," I responded.

Finally at noon, Halvorson concluded his cross-
examination and we recessed for lunch.

Chapter 40 – My Witnesses

The afternoon included the testimony of friends and colleagues of mine testifying on my behalf. I was confident that their testimony would be powerful and convincing. All of them were well respected and highly regarded in the work place and the community.

Our first witness was Bob Phipps. During the past couple of years Bob was a manager reporting to Benson. I had often consulted with Bob on various issues. We had established a good working relationship based on trust and respect. Bob was the only current BEA employee that I had requested to testify on my behalf. I knew that any employee who would dare to testify on my behalf would be risking their career to do so. I asked Bob because I believed he had the moral courage to tell the truth, even in the face of adversity.

After Bob reviewed his 35 years of laboratory experience, DeAnne asked him whether he had any prior experience with whistle blower complaints. Bob explained that in 2002, he was the manager of the legal function for Argonne National Laboratory West. He said that he had direct involvement with a prior DOE whistle blower. When asked, Bob told the court that it was appropriate for me to have written my DOE whistle blower complaint using government time and equipment. Bob testified that he informed Benson and me of his opinion in 2006.

Bob testified that he was interviewed by Torrance and questioned about the allegation that I had been biased in the performance of an investigation.

Bob said, "I felt he (Dennis) tried very hard to stay in the middle of that issue, that he was unbiased as

much as he possibly could, could be, and was trying to get
at the facts of the case."

When asked about his opinion of my character
Bob testified, "I believe he is a very honest individual who
has strong beliefs in, in what is right and ethical, and that
he would stick by those beliefs."

At the conclusion of Bob's testimony Adeyeye
asked Bob his opinion as to whether Benson and I could
work together again.

Bob replied, "I think they both would attempt to
make the situation work." Halvorson's cross examination
lasted only about ninety seconds and did nothing to
discredit Bob's testimony.

The next witness called by DeAnne was Phil
Wells. Phil had worked for Benson as an auditor from
August 2000 through May 2003.

When asked about my character Phil replied, "He
was extremely professional. He was well known to always
abide by any laws, rules, and professional ethics, whatever.
It was known that he, if anything, went to the extreme to
make sure that everything was abided by."

DeAnne asked Phil about his experience with
Benson.

Phil replied, "During my audits I was well known
for being very detailed. There are things that I began to
uncover that I felt were unallowable, if not illegal, as far as
reimbursement from the Federal Government. When I

raised these objections, Mr. Benson did everything to quiet me, to make sure I did not bring them up. As I continued to bring them up, he became more irate at that."

DeAnne asked Phil if Benson ever did anything to keep him from raising issues.

Phil replied, "He made the point that I would have to send emails to him rather than directly to managers. He then would go in and change those emails to what he wanted to say, and forward it to the manager as though I had written them."

DeAnne asked Phil if he believed I could be reinstated to the position as Employee Concerns/Ethics Officer and be effective.

Phil responded, "Absolutely."

Halverson's cross examination of Phil lasted less than two minutes and did nothing to detract from the credibility of his testimony. He noted that Phil sounded angry at Benson and asked if he was correct in his observation. Phil replied, "Yes, I feel he is a very dishonest individual."

After a brief recess, DeAnne called as a witness, Katherine Moriarty, senior counsel for BEA. Moriarty was a witness for BEA, but DeAnne had determined that she could provide information useful to our side. Early in her testimony Moriarty said she had been employed by BEA since February 2005. As she testified, it reminded me of something that DeAnne had shared with me shortly after I had contacted her to represent me. DeAnne told me that when BEA assumed the contract, Mark Olsen had offered her the job that Moriarty now held. Here we sat with BEA's first choice of legal counsel representing me and their second choice as a witness for our side.

Moriarty confirmed that on September 6, 2006 she sent me an email note admitting that it was appropriate for me to write my whistle blower complaint on my work computer and using work time. DeAnne also got Moriarty to admit that management, including senior BEA management was aware that I had filed the whistle blower complaint when they met to discuss the issues that led to my three day suspension in October 2006.

DeAnne questioned Moriarty extensively on the issue of my being one of only eleven employees in the entire laboratory who received a zero merit increase for calendar year 2006. This was a key element of my allegation that BEA had retaliated against me. Moriarty had been a good witness for our side.

It was now time for the testimony of John Denson. John held the position of President of the Laboratory from October 1994 through September 1999 when the lab was managed by Lockheed Martin. During this time, I reported directly to John. We had a great working relationship.

A year ago I had contacted John and told him of my situation.

"Is there anything I can do to help," he had asked.

I paused, before asking, "Would you be willing to fly out and testify on my behalf?"

"Yes, Dennis, I would be glad to testify about your character and integrity," he had responded.

DeAnne asked John to explain why the ethics office reported directly to him.

John replied, "It's the way Lockheed Martin's ethics program was set up. Each President was to have an ethics officer reporting directly to him but also with a dotted line responsibility to the corporation, which provided uniformity. And Dennis' job was to handle the ethics of our company, ethics problems of our company, and to report those to the corporation, and review those with me on at least a monthly basis." DeAnne went on to ask John about my performance. John replied that I was a good performer and had received a couple of promotions.

DeAnne asked about the issue of confidentiality.

John replied, "I wanted everyone to feel they could go to the ethics office and not have anything happen to them. Their identity didn't have to be revealed to anyone other than the ethics office."

DeAnne asked John if I ever had any conflict with senior management in the performance of my job. John replied yes, but noted that management knew that he was going to support the ethics office.

John stated, "I don't think there's any way he could have done the job and not made some of these guys angry, because we had a big organization. There were six thousand people and there was always some conflict."

DeAnne asked about my interaction with management, John replied, "I never got anything but real good news about him out of our management team. They didn't always agree with him but they knew he was doing the job as well as he could. And so --- I backed him on it."

DeAnne closed by asking John about my character.

John testified, "I wanted someone that would dig their heels in and do that job right, because it's the way Lockheed Martin operates. They want ethical conduct out of everybody. And since, the President's responsible for everything, well, I had to have somebody I thought was of high character and good moral standing and ethical background. He satisfied all those things for me."

As I listened to the testimony of my former boss I was humbled by his remarks. I was honored that he had taken the time to testify. To my knowledge, this was an unprecedented act. Never before, in a DOE whistleblower case, had a former President testified on behalf of the whistleblower. In my opinion, this spoke volumes about John's character and his commitment to doing the right thing.

Halvorson's cross examination lasted less than three minutes and did nothing to detract from the credibility of John's testimony.

The final witness called on my behalf was Joan Mehner. Joan was a good friend and had worked for me in the ethics office from 1997 through January 2005. Joan knew both Benson and me very well and could provide testimony about our individual character and integrity.

DeAnne asked Joan to describe me as a supervisor. Joan replied, "I would say he was probably one of the best managers I ever had in my whole career. I had one other that is outstanding and he is right up there with her."

Again, Halvorson's cross examination was brief and uneventful. Joan's testimony wrapped up things for the day. I left the courthouse feeling affirmed and more importantly blessed to have such positive people in my life, people of great courage and conviction.

Chapter 41 – Hearing, Day 3 - BEA Witnesses

The third day of the hearing, Thursday, November 29, 2007 I awoke with great anticipation and just a bit of trepidation. Today would be the testimony of my former boss, Doug Benson. Since 2005 I had come to see a side of Benson that others had told me about for years. The dishonesty, vengefulness, and self-serving nature of Benson's personality had come front and center. Today was my opportunity to see firsthand how he would answer questions when under oath, with the potential penalty of imprisonment.

Benson approached the bench with an exaggerated sense of authority. He glanced over at me. He raised his right hand and swore to tell the truth. Benson was asked about his responsibilities as the Director of Internal Audit. Benson stated that his organization was responsible for conducting independent reviews on behalf of management to ensure that management objectives were being met, that they were in compliance with laws, regulations, contract, and DOE Orders. He said that he was also responsible for the Employee Concerns Program.

Benson spent the next two hours describing my alleged misconduct and justifying his disciplinary actions against me.

When asked about the possibility of me being reinstated to the Employee Concerns Program, he responded, "I don't see how that could – I don't see how that could function." I was not surprised by his testimony,

it just reinforced the fact that BEA would do everything
possible to make sure that I would never again be the
Ethics Officer/Employee Concerns Manager for the INL.

Under cross-examination DeAnne asked Benson,
"When you first met Mr. Patterson, what was your
impression?"

Benson replied, "He was very professional."

"And you would agree that he was well respected
as the Ethics Officer and Employee Concerns Manager,
correct?"

Benson replied, "Yes."

DeAnne continued, "And I think you already
testified, too and you won't dispute that you evaluated Mr.
Patterson as Outstanding in the years prior to the 2006
evaluation, correct?"

"That's correct," Benson testified.

DeAnne asked Benson about the investigative
report authored by the Battelle Corporate Office in early
2006. DeAnne read from the report, "We recommend
that BEA senior management evaluate and identify actions
it considers appropriate to improve the working
relationship between the Ethics Office and the involved
managers and departments in this matter."

DeAnne continued, "Isn't it true that BEA senior
management did not take any action with regard to that
recommended action from Corporate?'

"Formal action? No, they did not" Benson said.

Deanne asked further, "So, is it true that senior management didn't take any specific action as was recommended in the Corporate Report?"

Benson replied, 'I didn't see individuals who this was addressed to take an action, no."

As I listened to this testimony it angered me to hear what I already knew. No one in senior management gave a rat's behind about me. It was egregious for BEA to totally ignore a recommendation from Battelle corporate. Their failure to do so didn't harm anyone, except me. I remembered the words from one of BEA's three principles of priorities, "respect and caring for our people." Words without action mean nothing, and that is what BEA had done for me, nothing.

In further addressing the corporate report, DeAnne asked Benson, "And would you agree with me that the report also indicates that Mr. Patterson is, indeed, a very skilled investigator?"

Benson replied, "Yes, it does say that."

DeAnne asked Benson about Olsen's opinion that it was inappropriate for me to write my whistleblower complaint on company time and equipment. Benson acknowledged that Olsen's opinion was wrong and that had I not fought this issue it would have posed a risk to BEA in future whistleblower actions. Benson also acknowledged that my actions led to policy changes that protected the rights of employees.

Halvorson asked Benson about my removal from the Ethics/Employee Concerns position.

- Halverson, "Was Mr. Patterson's refusal to disclose the name of the sources a factor in his directed reassignment?"
- Benson, "Not in my opinion; no."

Upon hearing what I knew was a lie, I conferred with DeAnne.

After Halverson concluded his examination, DeAnne began her cross examination. She handed Benson the letter authored and signed by him June 13, 2007.

- DeAnne, "If you will take a look at that document, second paragraph, "isn't it true that you specifically identify one of the actions that caused the directed reassignment was Mr. Patterson's failure to provide the name."
- Benson, "That's how this reads, yes."
- DeAnne, "No further questions."
- Halverson, nothing further."

We had caught Benson in a lie. His testimony was directly contradicted by a letter authored and signed by him. I wondered whether or not Adeyeye would take punitive action against Benson. I was almost certain that BEA wouldn't take any action.

The next to testify was the Security investigator. Torrance testified that Katherine Moriarty asked him to investigate me for misuse of government equipment in June 2006. He further testified it was Moriarty who asked him to investigate me a second time in August 2006 for alleged bias.

Torrance said that he had never before investigated anyone for bias and that it was not something Security would normally investigate.

Torrance testified that he filed a complaint against me on September 21, 2006. Torrance said he saw me walking behind him and assumed that my intent was to intimidate him. He testified that he contacted Zabala and reported me.

My new boss Ed Anderson, was called to the stand by Halvorson as a BEA witness. However, his testimony turned out to be more helpful to me. He testified that in our first meeting I raised questions about my qualifications for the job.

"Dennis was very clear that he was—He made the statement that he's going to be as good as he can be, whatever we've got for him to do. And he's done that. It's been comfortable, not combative at all." Ed also testified that prior to my being assigned to his organization he had never seen my resume.

Toni Vandel was called as a witness for BEA. She discussed her and Zabala's interrogation of me on May 16, 2007 in response to Middleton and Benson accusing me of improper conduct when they directed me on April 24th to disclose the confidential name.

When asked about my demeanor in the interview she replied, "He was very business-like, serious. He was not hostile, he was just there to answer the questions."

Vandel was asked about the disciplinary action meeting where it was decided I would be transferred to engineering. Vandel said that Zabala stated that I did not deny Middleton and Benson's allegations that I had treated them with disrespect. She said based on this information

130

they decided to remove me from the Ethics Office. Those
that participated in the disciplinary decision included
Benson, Zabala, Mark Holubar (HR director), Mark Olsen
and Art Clark.

When Zabala testified about my conduct in the same
May 16 meeting, she testified under oath, "He (Dennis
Patterson) was hostile and very condescending, and it was
difficult to talk with him."

So, while Vandel described me as business like, now I
was being described as hostile. Zabala testified that in the
discipline meeting three options were discussed,
termination, suspension and reassignment.

During testimony Zabala acknowledged that the
company did not have a written open door policy.

DeAnne asked Zabala about my alleged inappropriate
statements made to Benson and Middleton. Zabala stated
that I admitted making the statements. However, under
cross-examination she admitted that she never asked me if
I admitted or denied making the statements.

- DeAnne: "You'll agree that you never asked him
  to confirm or deny whether he made those
  statements?"
- Zabala: "No, I told him that those were the
  statements attributed to him in that meeting."

Earlier, when cross-examining Vandel, DeAnne
questioned her about BEA's attempt to equate my alleged
misconduct and discipline to another event. DeAnne got
Vandel to admit that one of the so called "similar events"
involved serious misconduct by Security officers.

In her testimony Vandel said, "The horseplay involved

the Security Department, and some individuals. You would liken it to something like hazing, like an initiation; individuals had been tied up, and then photographs taken with the guards." She testified it didn't include nudity. I smiled as I listened, because I had heard from several credible sources that this incident involved nudity, duct tape, and a gun.

Vandel failed in her attempt to equate my situation to this egregious act of misconduct by employees responsible for protecting the property and people of the INL.

The next BEA witness was Security investigator, Dyanna. Her testimony was important because she was the Security investigator that insisted I disclose the confidential source. Under cross-examination she noted that at the time the issue came up she had only been employed at the INL for 17 days. Specific to the issue of confidentiality the following questions and answers occurred between DeAnne and Dyanna:

- DeAnne, "Well, isn't it true that you had received an email from not just Mr. Patterson, but Mr. Benson, --
- Dyanna, "um-hum
- DeAnne, "-- saying that confidentiality could not be breached"
- Dyanna, "I did receive those emails, yes."
- DeAnne, "And still, based on that direction from his up-line management, you still believed that Mr. Patterson was failing to cooperate with your investigation?"
- Dyanna, "I still believe to this day that Mr. Patterson failed to cooperate with my investigation."
- DeAnne, "And do you have any support from your supervisors toward that opinion?"

- Dyanna, "My supervisor, …Mr. Middleton"

It was now turn for my former friend and neighbor, Security Director, Tom Middleton to testify. By now, I had come to expect the worst from Middleton and so I thought nothing was going to surprise me. I was wrong!

Middleton was asked about whether he supported Dyanna's insistence that I disclose the name of the confidential source. Middleton said he did and that was the reason he was in the April 16, 2007 meeting with Benson and myself.

DeAnne got Middleton to admit that Dyanna had interviewed the confidential source prior to April 16, 2007, and that I had arranged for the anonymous phone call. Nonetheless, Middleton was absolute in asserting that there was no other option other than for me to disclose the confidential name and that my failure to do so was unacceptable. He went on to describe me in the harshest of terms.

- Halvorson, "Do you believe you could work effectively with Patterson if he were reinstated to the position of Employee Concerns Program Manager?
- Middleton, "I would have to say I cannot." "The other grave concern is Dennis rejected his manager's authority over him…an investigator who has come to the conclusion that he's above the law, that he has no authority over him is a person who is going to hurt people unnecessarily…the license to investigate without management oversight is where you get the

Gestapo." There was an audible gasp from the courtroom when Middleton used the word Gestapo.

- DeAnne, in cross-examination, read from my email, "I am willing to contact the employee and ask her if she would be willing to sit down with Dyanna and/or call Dyanna a second time…anonymously and visit with her."

- DeAnne asked Middleton why this wasn't an acceptable option vs. forcing me to disclose the confidential name.

- Middleton replied, "With that proposal the problem is I don't know what the source said. I don't know what the source has actually said."

Middleton provided no credible explanation for why he and Benson had tried to force me to disclose a confidential source.

DeAnne read for Middleton an email that Benson wrote when Security initially requested the identity of the confidential source, "Confidentiality is required by the Employee Concern Order, as with my other investigative process. We cannot breach that requirement. The employee must make their decision."

Middleton testified that he only learned of this email from Benson a few days ago, but that it didn't change his opinion.

During Middleton's direct examination he stated that he felt threatened by some of our interactions such as my not speaking to him in the hall, supposedly staring at him from across the street, and allegedly cutting him off as we left our driveways. Appallingly, he said that he was concerned for the safety of his family. Under cross-examination the following exchange occurred:

- DeAnne, "And you asserted that you had to question whether this might be a risk for your family, is that right?"
- Middleton, "I felt like my family – I was worried that my family was at risk. I didn't know."
- DeAnne, "Well, isn't it true that your daughter and Mr. Patterson's daughter are friends?"
- Middleton, "Yes they go to school together and have been friends for ten years.
- DeAnne, "And isn't it true that after that time, that you still allowed your daughter to go over to his home?"
- Middleton, "I did"
- DeAnne, "Even though you had this fear?"
- Middleton, "I allowed them to go to school together too; yea"

In one breath he said that he was afraid that I might harm his family and in the next he admitted to allowing his daughter to come over to our home unsupervised. I looked at the hearing officer as Middleton testified on this subject, even she seemed to be taken aback by his testimony.

Moriarty was called to the stand by Halvorson. Moriarty testified that she was the person who requested that I be investigated for misuse of property in June 2006. She noted that she had earlier advised me about a "prohibition against using government time to pursue personal matters."

She further testified, "When the Idaho Human Rights Commission contacted me and told me that Mr. Patterson was asking to withdraw his complaint, I asked the IHRC investigator for more details. She indicated, 'Well I can just send you those. He (Dennis) sent those (emails) to me from his government computer. I'll just forward those to you.' And so when I received those emails I looked at them and was very surprised, because I understood that Patterson had agreed with me that he was not going to use government time or equipment to pursue this personal claim…it was at that point I decided an investigation was necessary."

This testimony illustrated some of the craziness that had occurred. Moriarty just testified that she had me investigated for misuse of government equipment even though she knew the reason I sent the emails was to request dismissal of my discrimination complaint. This confirmed, in my mind, that the real reason she had me investigated was because she had learned I had filed my whistleblower complaint.

Under questioning by DeAnne, Moriarty acknowledged that shortly after April 15th, 2007 she pulled my emails and thereby identified the name of the confidential employee. Benson and Middleton simply used my refusal to breach confidentiality as a reason to remove me from the Ethics/Employee Concerns office.

Chapter 42 – The Close

Friday, the last day of the hearing, I was looking forward to DeAnne's closing argument. In the trial scenes I had seen on TV, the closing arguments always made for great drama. Unfortunately, it was late in the day when testimony from BEA's witnesses concluded. DeAnne and Halvorson agreed to forego the closing arguments with the stipulation that they would file closing briefs at a later date.

At 4:53 p.m. Adeyeye adjourned the hearing. I put my
arm around LaVonna and held her close. I remembered
one of my favorite scriptures, Proverbs 10, 9 "A man of
integrity walks securely, but he who takes a crooked path
will be found out." I believed that my integrity withstood
the attacks from BEA and that light had been shed on the
unjust actions of Benson, Middleton, Olsen and others.
God had answered our prayers.

DeAnne and Halvorson shook hands like two fighters
at the end of a championship match. Halvorson
whispered to DeAnne, "excellent job of finding all our
weaknesses." To hear one attorney make that admission
to another attorney, seemed odd. It was, however,
reassuring. DeAnne had performed exceptionally well.
We were an awesome team.

I shook hands with Adeyeye and said, "Thanks for
what you do. I hope you enjoyed your time in Idaho
Falls."

"Well, it was quite an experience, I've never been part
of a hearing with so much media coverage," she replied.

Someone handed her copies of the newspaper articles
published during the week. As Adeyeye prepared to leave
the room I overheard a reporter ask when a decision
would be rendered.

"In approximately 30 to 60 days," she said. This
meant we would have an answer by the end of January,
2008.

Chapter 43 – The Witness Who Wasn't

A couple of months prior to the hearing I was hopeful that a very important witness would testify on my behalf. This person had been the DOE-Idaho Employee Concerns Program Manager from approximately 2000 through the middle of 2005. His role and responsibility included oversight of the BEA Employee Concerns Program. Over the years we had developed a strong professional relationship and friendship. His father was a very good friend of mine and had been my mentor for a number of years earlier in my career.

In August 2007, I asked him to meet me in the company cafeteria. We had a cup of coffee and I updated him on my whistleblower case. Throughout our discussion, he expressed confidence in the process as well as his respect for me. After several minutes, I mustered the courage to ask, "Would you be willing to testify at the hearing as a character witness?"

"I would be glad to, I don't see a problem, DOE doesn't have a dog in the fight" he replied. He paused, then added, "Well, maybe I better check with legal before I commit."

"Thanks, this really means a lot to me, please get back to me as soon as possible," I said.

Over the next couple of days I didn't hear from him and so I decided to send an email. In his response, he informed me that after speaking to DOE-ID legal he determined that DOE-ID did indeed "have a dog in the fight."

He said, "I better not testify on your behalf because it might seem as though I would be taking a position contrary to DOE."

I was disappointed because the testimony of the
former manager of the DOE-Idaho Employee Concerns
Program would have been powerful. His response,
confirmed my suspicion that DOE-Idaho was not the
independent overseer that it was supposed to be. My
thoughts went back to the fall of 2005 when the DOE
attorney sent me the email note. DOE had sided with
Mark Olsen on the subject of my writing my whistleblower
complaint on my work computer. DOE-ID was
supposed to be the safeguard for ensuring INL was
operated safely, effectively and in compliance with
regulations. In my opinion, DOE-ID was not fulfilling its
duty to the American taxpayer. Instead, it was protecting
BEA, and its own self-interest.

Chapter 44 – More Headlines

On the front page of the Post Register, December
1, 2007, Middleton was quoted as saying he couldn't work
with me if I was reinstated in my former position.

On December 4, 2007 there was a front page
headline, "DOE Fines Battelle." The article noted that
DOE had fined BEA $123,750 for "violating the federal
agency's nuclear safety requirements." DOE charged BEA
with failure to adhere to technical safety requirements and
reactor operating instructions. BEA was also cited for
inadequacies in the reactor operation instructions, failure
to correct known problems with a reactor component, and
failure to adequately conduct management assessments.

The subject manager was guilty of restarting a nuclear reactor without following procedure. Yet, his discipline was only four days off without pay. During my hearing BEA had brought this issue up with the intent to demonstrate that how they disciplined me was no different than how they disciplined other employees. Of course, no reasonable person would equate improperly starting a nuclear reactor with my supposed misconduct. The manager's actions created a potential danger to the INL, the environment and the surrounding community.

On December 7, 2007 there was another front page story. While this incident had nothing to do with the INL, it was another example of an employee who had fought against injustice and won. The headline announced a victim of sexual harassment had been awarded, by a federal jury, a total of $466,250. Jurors found the person had been the victim of a sexually hostile work environment and that the perpetrator had committed both assault and battery upon her. This was a courageous individual that refused to be harassed and intimidated. And like myself, she was represented by an attorney that believed in her cause. That attorney was, DeAnne Casperson.

On January 16, 2008 the front page read, "Idaho Falls Group is Dreaming Big." The article referenced the upcoming Dr. Martin Luther King banquet. The article stated, "Two summers ago, a group of Idaho Falls residents took King's creed to heart and formed the African American Alliance." The proceeds of the banquet were to benefit a young teenager who had recently been diagnosed with a life threatening condition. The AAA also gave college scholarships to African American graduating high school seniors.

Chapter 45 –"We Should Not Be Deterred"

I was looking forward to the 2008 Dr. King
banquet. Anthony Hebron was our keynote speaker.
Hebron was a corporate executive vice president for
Battelle Memorial Institute. He was flying to Idaho Falls
on a Battelle corporate jet and I would be meeting him at
the Aeromark airport. As I waited in the lobby, I
wondered if Hebron had any knowledge of my whistle
blower complaint. It was likely that someone from BEA
had told him about it. As I gazed out the window, I saw
the jet land and begin coasting up to the small airport
lobby. I watched as it slowly taxied to a stop. The steps to
the jet slowly deployed.

The first person who stepped off the plane was
Anthony. As he reached the bottom of the steps I saw
another person exit the plane. It was Grossenbacher.

In December I had asked him to say a few words
at the MLK banquet. He initially accepted. Then, with no
explanation, his office contacted me and told me he
wouldn't be able to attend. Now, here he was walking
towards the airport lobby with Anthony. I expected
Grossenbacher to enter with Hebron and do the
introductions.

Fifteen feet from the door, Grossenbacher took a
left turn and disappeared. I couldn't believe it. Sitting
together on the small jet, surely Anthony told him I was
waiting for him. Yet, Grossenbacher chose to leave
without even a, "hello." I walked to the entrance and

welcomed Anthony.

As we drove to the hotel, Anthony asked me what it was like to live in Idaho Falls. I told him it was a great place to raise a family. I told Anthony about a discrimination incident that had occurred at the INL several years ago. After listening to the situation he remarked, "Dennis it is sad that such things continue to happen in today's world." I was tempted to tell him I was a whistle blower and that discrimination was part of the story, but I thought better of it.

When Anthony and I entered the banquet room I was pleased to see the room filled to capacity. Anthony and I took our seats at the head table. Seated to my left was Anthony and to his left, Beth Sellers, Manager of DOE, Idaho. This was a rare occasion – a whistleblower, an executive from the company's corporate office, and a DOE senior manager, dining together.

Unbeknownst to anyone but a handful of us, there was another interesting situation in the room. Mayor Fuhriman was seated at a table just to my right. He was seated at the table with the members of his newly formed "Race Relations Committee." The mayor had created the committee to improve race relations in Idaho Falls.

The Vice-Chair was the director of BEA's Protective Force Security organization. Two days earlier, I learned that he had just been suspended without pay by Middleton for allegedly pointing a gun at a colleague's head and threatening to kill him. The director had called me over the holidays and told me a different version. He told me there was a gun involved but he never pointed it at anyone and it was just part of some horseplay. He explained that he and the colleague were good friends and it happened at the person's home.

Meanwhile, everyone at the Mayor's table, including the Vice Chair, were laughing and having a great time. The mayor had no idea that his Vice-Chair would soon be fired by BEA.

Less than two years ago, Middleton had announced that he had selected this person to manage more than 250 Protective Force employees. At the time, I was pleased that an African American had been chosen for such an important position.

A few days after the banquet he was terminated. My understanding was the alleged gun incident was a key factor in the decision to terminate him. If this was true, I wondered why this issue was never reported to the police or local news.

Anthony began his keynote address, "Dr. King was an extraordinary man and a humble man. The night before he was gunned down he asked people to remember him not for his honors or awards, but for how he helped his fellow man. Dr. King was a man of great faith…operating in that faith he left a challenge for us and that challenge is to abandon the comfort of complacency." He went on to discuss the importance of diversity in the highest echelons of agencies and organizations. Anthony challenged individuals to "do the best job you can," and organizations to take actions that result in measurable progress. Anthony concluded his speech with, "We still have a lot of work ahead, and we've got some risks we all have to take. But we must remember that back in the 60's that vision of night sticks, demon dogs, and Sheriff Bull Connor's minions attacking civil rights workers, those were Dr. King's followers. Those actions did not deter them and we should not be deterred now." At the end of the evening, while shaking Anthony's hand, I said, "I was inspired and encouraged by your talk tonight, one day I will be able to tell you why." One day I would tell him about the challenges and risk of being a whistleblower.

Chapter 46 – Yes We Can

Senator Barack Obama had just won the Iowa Primary. It seemed that America was open to electing its first African American president. I was telling family, friends, and colleagues that Obama was the best person to lead our country. Of course, making such statements in one of the reddest states was not always well received. Nonetheless, I was a believer,

When LaVonna and I heard that Obama was going to be in Boise on Saturday, February 2, there was no way we would miss seeing him. We heard on the news that more than 10,000 were expected. Half-jokingly, I told LaVonna that I was going to shake his hand. We arrived in Boise the night before and stayed with my sister Lou.

The next morning the family was up early. We arrived at the Taco Bell Arena before 6:00 a.m. There were already hundreds of people in line. It did my heart good to see such an incredible turnout for an African American Democrat in Idaho. The atmosphere in the arena was like being at a rock concert.

Obama walked onto the raised platform. Music played loud and the sense of anticipation was palpable. Obama smiled and waved to the crowd.

"And they told me there weren't any Democrats in Idaho, but I did not believe them, I did not believe them." The roar of approval was deafening.

Obama commented that his hope for the future of America was an important part of his message. He said that people were beginning to call him a "hope monger." The crowd erupted with laughter. I listened intently to his dream of a better America. His message of "Yes we can," and an America that was inclusive instead of exclusive was invigorating.

Obama ended with, "This is our moment, this is our time…We will remake this country and together we will remake the world." I felt energized, empowered and encouraged.

As he ended his speech, LaVonna said, "Why don't you go down and see if you can shake his hand." Without pause, I gave her a peck on the cheek and ran down the steps.

As I approached the stadium floor, I couldn't see Obama. Then, I spotted a boom microphone moving along in front of the crowd. Keeping an eye on the microphone, I moved people aside, gently most of the time. Finally, I saw him. He was shaking hands with anyone who got their hand close to him. When I got just to the right of him, I stood on my tiptoes and reached my hand over the outstretched hands of several others.

As he passed in front of me I yelled, "Barack." Our eyes met for a fleeting moment. He reached out and shook my hand. It was a firm handshake, one that I wouldn't soon forget.

I couldn't believe my good fortune. Of the more than fourteen thousand people at the rally I was one of the lucky few. It was definitely a special moment. I couldn't wait to get back to Lavonna and tell her that I shook the hand of our future president.

When we finally got back together, the smile on her face told me that she already knew. She saw me shake his hand.

As we made our way to the exit a young lady ran up behind us and grabbed the sleeve of my coat, "Hey, I think I saw you shake Obama's hand." Yep, I did," I said.

"Can I shake your hand? I want to tell my friends, I shook the hand of a man that shook Obama's." I gave her a firm handshake and a smile.

What a great ending to a great experience. LaVonna commented that the only thing she regretted was that she was so excited that she forgot to take a picture. I told her it didn't matter because I had the memory of the moment. Our family and friends would just have to believe us when we told the story.

The next day my sister Lou called and told me that my picture, reaching out to shake Obama's hand was in the Boise paper, the Idaho Statesman.

Chapter 47 – A Trade?

In early 2008, I learned that one of the BEA senior managers, Dwayne Coburn, was romantically involved with an administrative support person in his organization. Apparently the two of them had recently disclosed the relationship. As a result, she was transferred to Internal Audit. This was the same organization that I

had been transferred out of in June 2007. Coburn was the
director of the engineering organization that I was
transferred to. Perhaps, Coburn did a favor for Benson
and now Benson was doing a favor for Coburn. I wonder
to this day, if this is what happened.

Rumor had it that Coburn's "friend" was receiving
special treatment. Her cubicle was modified with taller
cubicle walls and a doorway. I later learned that she didn't
have to interview for the position and that the supervisor
(under Benson) didn't even know she had been hired until
she returned from vacation. It all seemed very odd and as
a result rumors were running rampant. I heard that
someone had reported the relationship and the alleged
favoritism to Grossenbacher and the Department of
Energy Inspector General's Office.

Chapter 48 – Discouragement & Encouragement

Hearing Officer Adeyeye did not render the
decision within the projected 30 to 60 days. For all we
knew, the decision could be made today, tomorrow or
months from now. DOE had the power to grant itself
extension after extension without any recourse. All we
could do was wait.

In late February, I heard that BEA was in the
process of hiring a new Employee Concerns Program
Manager. She was from the Hanford Washington area and
was moving to Idaho Falls in March. I believed that BEA
was hiring her at this time to strengthen their case for not

reinstating me in the position. BEA had argued at the hearing that I should not be reinstated. They had also showed evidence that attempted to explain why the Ethics/Employee Concerns position had been downgraded two levels and made into a part time position. By filling the position before DOE OHA issued the decision, they could also argue that it would create a hardship on the newly hired employee.

In early March, I walked by my old office and saw a new nameplate on the door. It was disheartening to see someone else sitting at my desk after occupying the office for the past thirteen years. Over the next several weeks, I was in communication with my friends in the Internal Audit organization. They told me that the new person was not happy in her role as Employee Concerns Manager. Supposedly, she felt like BEA had misrepresented the job and job duties. As it turned out, she was only with BEA a few months. I was told that one day she walked in, submitted her resignation to Benson and left the same day.

With increasing regularity, I had to take a few hours of personal leave just to make it through the week. The stress of waiting for the decision from DOE and the worry of what else could go wrong was getting unbearable.

In the spring of 2008 LaVonna and I joined a prayer and study group at our church. We met weekly to study scripture, pray, and encourage each other. LaVonna and I shared our personal and work struggles. Our friends opened up their hearts to us and became our prayer warriors.

Chapter 49 – This Is It

The DOE OHA decision was now due to be issued in April, 2008. I was excited about the timing in part because my birthday was April 14. Unfortunately my birthday came and went without any response from the hearing officer. Each subsequent week began with hope and ended with disappointment.

On June 13, I sat in my cubicle and reflected upon my work life. Exactly a year ago, I had been involuntarily transferred to my current position in engineering. It had been a difficult time, but I had performed well and received a good performance appraisal. I was thankful that my new management had treated me well and given me the chance to succeed. However, the job was still a very poor match for my skills and abilities. My passion was helping employees, not pretending to be an engineer. Waiting day by day for the hearing officer's decision, while working in such conditions, was taking its toll.

June 20, 2008 was a beautiful day with white fluffy clouds scudding across a deep blue sky. LaVonna and I had to drive to Boise to pick up Jasmine. Jasmine had spent the prior few days at church camp, a hundred miles north of Boise. We had been on the interstate for only about twenty minutes when my cell phone rang. I looked at the caller ID.

"Sweetheart, it's DeAnne, I think this is it," I said.

"Hello," I answered breathlessly.

"Dennis, we just received the decision from Adeyeye," DeAnne said calmly.

149

"We won!" She proclaimed.

" LaVonna we won," I yelled as I reached over and grabbed her hand.

My heart felt like it was going to burst and I was grinning ear to ear.

I pulled into a rest area. DeAnne continued, "The report found that BEA retaliated against you on five separate occasions, concluding with removing you from the position of Ethics Officer."

"DeAnne, thank you, this feels so good," I replied.

I jumped out of the car and ran around to the other side. I grabbed LaVonna in my arms, lifted her off the ground and yelled, "God is so good sweetheart."

As I looked around, I could see people looking at us, probably wondering what was going on and why we were celebrating in the parking lot of a rest area. We held hands as we walked around the grassy area of the rest stop. It felt so good being together when we received the news. There is nothing like having the person you love share in the joys of life.

As we left the rest area, I remembered that I had told Sven Berg, the reporter for the Post Register, that I would call him when I received the decision. I called and told him the results.

He asked for my thoughts on the outcome. I told him, "I was confident from day one. I believed that the hearing officer would make the right decision and this would be to the benefit of many people besides myself."

Sven said that the story would appear in the

newspaper the following morning. I was pleased that the
information would be published so quickly. It was
important for the Idaho Falls community and even the rest
of the country to know what had happened.

As we continued the drive, the green fields
seemed to be greener, the blue sky bluer and the white
clouds whiter. When we arrived at the Nazarene Church I
could see Jasmine anxiously waiting for us. It was good to
see her pretty smiling face after being away for several
days. I decided to wait until we got home to tell her the
good news. It was great just to listen to her excitedly tell
about the happenings at church camp. The stories left no
doubt that it had been a fun and rewarding experience.

Upon arriving home we shared the good news
with Jasmine and Darius. We had a big family hug and the
kids told me how proud they were of me. For the first
time in a long time, it felt like all was well.

Later that evening I logged onto my computer so I
could read the entirety of the DOE OHA decision. As
DeAnne had explained, the letter contained the following:

- The security investigation of me for "bias" was
  retaliation.
- The 3 day suspension in October 2006 was
  retaliation.
- The low performance appraisal dated January 10,
  2007 was retaliation.
- The zero merit increase for 2006 was retaliation.
- Removing me from the Ethics/Employee
  Concerns position was retaliation.

The decision directed BEA to do the following:

- Remove suspension notice and poor performance appraisal from my personnel file.
- Provide a retroactive merit increase for 2006.
- Reimburse lost pay for participating in the hearing proceedings.
- Reimbursement for attorney fees.
- Within 30 days of decision, BEA shall notify Patterson if there is a vacancy comparable to Patterson's previous position.

Unfortunately, the hearing officer did not require BEA to reinstate me in the Ethics/Employee concerns position. The decision cited the fact that the position had been modified and had been lowered from a specialist 5 to a 4 or 3. The decision stated, "As senior/auditor/employee concerns manager under Benson's new position, Patterson would be subject to an even lower salary scale and would be effectively demoted."

The report contained the following notation, "However, if Patterson so chooses, he should be considered for rotation into this position, especially in light of BEA's expressed desire to salvage his career at INL."

Note 19 of the report stated, "Some of the complaints against Patterson's behavior seem exaggerated." "There is no evidence in the record of aggressive, threatening behavior by Patterson."

The report also contained the following notation regarding the Summary Judgment granted to BEA on November 21, 2007 – "As noted in Section I.B., I dismissed this complaint on procedural grounds. Nonetheless, it appears, based on the findings of the ROI, that there was substantive merit to the disclosures, which alleged an abuse of authority related to violations of company procedure. The focus of this Decision is not, however, on the allegations contained in the first complaint but on those alleged retaliatory actions that occurred after Patterson filed his first (whistleblower) complaint, as the mere filing of this complaint constituted protected conduct under Part 708." This was a direct reference to the actions of BEA in the Loren site access matter in 2005.

As midnight approached, I couldn't sleep. The excitement of the day was still with me and my thoughts continued to race. I decided to send an email to all my friends and supporters to let them know the good news. I went into my office, just down from our master bedroom, and began preparing the message. My hands were shaking as I typed. I told everyone of DOE's decision and thanked them for their support. The email went out to close to a hundred individuals across the country, from California to North Carolina.

The next morning I awoke early. As I walked out to get the newspaper I felt this deep appreciation for life and the goodness of life. As I picked up the paper I looked at the front page. The headline, "DOE Finds in Favor of INL Employee"

Chapter 50 – Justice Delayed

BEA did not respond with integrity. Instead, the following Monday, June 23, the INL Communications Department issued the following iNote, "We believe that we acted appropriately and fairly in the case of Mr.

Patterson when he filed three complaints against the company between June and October 2006. A decision concerning a possible appeal from the ruling is pending."

In the face of DOE's decision, BEA continued to maintain it had done no wrong.

In spite of this, I felt vindicated and validated. Of course, the good feelings were tempered by the possibility that BEA might appeal. According to the DOE letter, BEA had 15 days to decide.

On day thirteen, July 3, 2008 LaVonna, Jasmine and I flew to Myrtle Beach, SC to spend the holiday with LaVonna's family. On Independence Day we had a big barbeque and watched the fireworks on the beach. The next couple of days were relaxing, but I knew that things could change in the blink of an eye.

On the morning of July 7th I awoke early and took a walk around the resort. I stopped by the small café, got a cup of coffee and returned to our room. I joined LaVonna out on the balcony. We talked about the great time we were having. Just then my cell phone rang.

"It's DeAnne," I told LaVonna.

"Hello Dennis," DeAnne said. I could tell by the sound of her voice that it wasn't good news. She continued, "BEA is appealing DOE's decision."

After finishing the call, I held LaVonna's hand. "It's not over, BEA is appealing," I told her. I explained the appeal process and what it meant to our future. I told her that it could be several months before DOE would make a determination.

I barely had time to digest the news when I received a call from Sven Berg. He wanted my response to

the appeal. I told him, "I am fully confident that
Adeyeye's ruling will be upheld. BEA can't change the
facts."

Despite the bad news, I was determined that
nothing would keep us from enjoying our vacation. I
focused on the goodness of life instead of the hardship
ahead.

When I returned to work it was weird knowing
everything that had transpired while I was away. While in
Myrtle Beach the Post Register ran a front page story with
the headline, "Appeal is Filed in Whistle-blower Case."
Additionally, BEA issued an iNote on July 8, 2008. The
iNote was issued by Olsen with "concurrence" from
Grossenbacher.

The iNote said in part, "We have chosen to appeal
the decision because, among other reasons, we believe that
(i) the hearing officer's findings of fact and conclusions of
law, in several instances, are conflicting, and (ii) the
conclusions of retaliation are against the weight of the
evidence presented at the hearing...litigation is a lousy way
to resolve disputes; but, when litigation occurs, we prefer
to try the case in the court having jurisdiction over the
particular case, rather than trying the case in the 'court of
public opinion' or the media. However, when the media
becomes heavily involved, we are going to respond
appropriately to make clear why we have selected the
particular course of action in question."

I was surprised at the tone of the iNote. In my
opinion there was a not so subtle message: any employee
that files a whistle blower complaint against the company
will be fought to the very end. I provided a copy to

DeAnne. She too was disturbed by the iNote and commented that the note itself appeared to be an act of retaliation.

Chapter 51 – A New Friend

After the decision I received many phone calls and emails of support from individuals throughout the community. One evening I received a phone call from a former employee of the city of Idaho Falls, Ed Turner. Ed had once been the city engineer for Idaho Falls. When he refused to follow illegal and unethical directions from city leadership, he became the victim of retaliation. Ed shared the following brief history of his whistleblower journey.

Ed had been a highly regarded and well respected engineer with the City of Idaho Falls for more than 27 years. As the city engineer Ed was eminently qualified and was licensed by the State of Idaho as a Professional Engineer and Land Surveyor.

In 1996 he was unceremoniously demoted and replaced by someone without city engineering experience and not licensed by the State. This person then directed Ed to approve plans and other engineering documents over which Ed did not have 'responsible charge.' Ed refused, because doing so would be in violation of the Idaho Engineering Licensing Statute and other regulations and ultimately would put the public at risk.

Ed's career suffered almost immediately. His work environment became so hostile that he resigned from his position. Upon loss of his job he sued the City of Idaho Falls for wrongful termination and breach of contract. Because of errors of his attorney, Ed lost his

fight with the city. Ed then sued his former attorney for
malpractice and in doing so was able to successfully prove
his case against the city and his first attorney. As with
most whistleblowers this long ordeal (more than 4 years)
came with unimaginable emotional, psychological and
financial consequences. But for Ed it was worth the price
– he had a moral and ethical obligation to protect the
public health and safety and he did so. In 1999 the
American Engineering Alliance of New York,
www.aeaworld.org presented him the 'Vanguard Award' –
"For extraordinary courage, dedication, initiative and
perseverance, demonstrating at great personal risk a path
toward elevating the engineering profession and
safeguarding the public interest." After hanging up, I
knew that I had just made a new friend.

Chapter 52 – Audacity

On July 17, 2008 I received a copy of BEA's
appeal letter to DOE OHA. DeAnne and I had
speculated on what grounds they might appeal and what
specific issues they would contest. We figured they might
challenge a few of the more substantive decisions of the
hearing officer. As it turned out, BEA used classic big
corporate strategy; concede nothing and contest
everything. The 148 page appeal letter stated that the
hearing officer "erred" on sixty different occasions.
DeAnne and I believed this was an abuse of the DOE
process. Responding to such a lengthy brief was going to
be exhaustive, costly and would substantially delay the
appeal decision. If the purpose was to wear me down it

wasn't going to work. DeAnne and I put together a response that we believed would shine a light on the abusive practices of BEA.

On August 8, BEA sent out the following iNote announcement, "Doug Benson, INL Director of Audits, will begin a six month professional development opportunity at Battelle Memorial Institute in Columbus Ohio effective mid-September. Upon completion of the assignment at Battelle Columbus, Doug will have the opportunity to return to INL or assume a position with BMI or another of its affiliates."

DOE had found Benson guilty of retaliation and instead of getting disciplined he got an assignment at corporate with all the perks. I took a deep breath, turned off my computer and went for a walk.

On October 6, 2008, employees received a special announcement. The iNote read, "DOE Special Assessment: BEA to retain INL contract to 2014." My stomach churned as I read DOE-ID manager, Beth Seller's statement, "I'm very encouraged by the performance of BEA, its management and you – the employees – in these key transitional years of the laboratory." The iNote included Grossenbacher's response, "To me, the message is that we are here to stay."

The thought that BEA "was here to stay" made me almost throw up. I had been through so much already and this added insult to injury.

It became increasingly difficult for me, as I waited for DOE to render a decision on BEA's appeal. DeAnne had responded to BEA's appeal on October 6. A couple weeks later we received an email from OHA that stated the case would be issued within 60 days. The estimated date was January 12, 2009.

Chapter 53 – The Time Has Come

Every day at work seemed to get longer. Pretending to be an engineer was exhausting. I began taking more hours of vacation. With the election getting closer I became obsessed with following the campaigns. I sat mesmerized for each debate and followed the daily polling. I had little doubt that America would soon elect its first African American President. The conversations at work inevitably turned political. I was only one of a handful of Obama supporters. I enjoyed telling my Republican friends that the time had come.

LaVonna, Jasmine and Darius were almost as excited as I was. On the evening of November 4, 2008 we gathered around the TV and watched the results come in. I had predicted that it would be an early victory. At 9:00 p.m. NBC's Bryan Williams proclaimed, "And we have news, there will be young children in the White House for the first time since the Kennedy generation, an African American has broken the barrier as old as the republic, an astonishing candidate, an astonishing campaign, a seismic shift in American politics, you are looking at the 44th president of the Unites States, the celebrations begin." The celebration had begun at our house. We high fived, jumped, hugged and shouted, "yes we can." I never thought I would see this day.

Chapter 54 – 2009 MLK Banquet

The first couple of weeks of 2009 went by slowly. The work days dragged on. Holding meetings and updating procedures filled my days. There was nothing satisfying or rewarding about my work. The thing that kept me motivated was the upcoming Dr. King banquet, being held on Saturday, January 19. Our keynote speaker was William Magwood IV. Bill had been the director of Nuclear Energy for DOE from 1998 through May 2005. Because of his close tie to the INL, we expected a large turnout of BEA senior managers.

The AAA had decided to invite the mayor of Rexburg, Idaho. Rexburg had been in the national news in November 2008 for a rather embarrassing event. The day after Barack Obama won the general election there were several children on a school bus that had chanted, "Assassinate Obama."

I picked up the phone and dialed the number of the mayor's office.

"Mayor Shawn Larsen", he answered.

"Good afternoon, my name is Dennis Patterson, president of the African American Alliance," I said.

The silence was deafening. I wasn't sure if he was still on the phone. I speculated that he was worried that I was calling to discuss the chanting incident and perhaps even threatening legal action.

"Yes, how may I help you," he finally responded.

"I'm calling to invite you to a banquet to honor
Dr. King," I said.

"I would love to," he practically blurted out. The
relief was evident in his voice.

A couple days prior to the banquet,
Grossenbacher's office asked for my help in arranging a
meeting with Bill Magwood. For a moment, I was
tempted to say thanks but no thanks. Instead, I replied,
"I'd be glad to."

The DOE OHA appeal decision was due on
Monday, January 12, but we still hadn't heard anything.
The day before the banquet I was both anxious and
excited. The next twenty four hours could be life
changing. Before going to work, I prayed for peace of
mind and a calm spirit. The work day was fairly routine. I
tried to stay focused on the work at hand, but my thoughts
would return to the impending DOE decision. The
decision was now three days past due. I thought about
BEA senior management. Surely, they too were worried
about the pending decision.

As lunch time approached, my cell phone rang
and I anxiously looked at the caller ID, it was DeAnne's
assistant, Brandi.

"We heard from the DOE Office of Hearings and
Appeals," she said. I held my breath as I waited for the
rest of the story. "DOE has given themselves an
extension, the new date is February 10," she continued.

The disappointment was overwhelming. I
thanked Brandi and ended the call. I took several deep
breaths, and tried to relax. It was so exasperating to have

justice delayed once again. BEA's strategy had worked. They had overwhelmed DOE with paperwork. I called LaVonna and gave her the news. "There must be a purpose beyond our understanding," she replied. She spoke with such conviction that it restored my confidence.

The next morning the AAA met with Magwood at Grandpa's Southern BBQ, a restaurant owned by my good friend, Lloyd Westbrook. Lloyd had worked at the INL but when Lockheed Martin offered a severance package back in the mid-nineties he followed his dream and opened the first African American owned restaurant in Idaho Falls. As he often said, the place where you can get the best ribs, greens and sweet potato pie west of the Mississippi.

Magwood expressed great interest in the AAA and our community. We discussed issues ranging from diversity to nuclear energy. After breakfast I drove him over to the INL and introduced him to Dr. Dave Hill, Deputy Laboratory Director for Science and Technology.

Later, I picked up Magwood and took him to the banquet. During the social hour I looked up and saw Grossenbacher. As he approached, he shook hands with Dave Snell. I watched as they chatted for a few minutes.

Grossenbacher walked towards me and extended his hand. We greeted each other with a firm grip.

"Great turnout Dennis, thanks to you and Dave for putting this on," he said. "Thank you for coming," I replied.

Finally, Grossenbacher and I had met face to face. This was our first opportunity to see each other as individuals rather than enemies engaged in battle. I hoped that this personal exchange might alter the future.

As the program kicked off, LaVonna and I took
our places at the head table along with Magwood. Others
at the table included: Dr. Hill; Mayor Fuhriman and wife;
John Kotek, former Deputy Manager DOE-ID and Ray
Furstenau, Deputy Manager, DOE-ID.

At a table next to us were members of BEA senior
management, Alavarez (named in my original whistle
blower complaint), Art Clark, K.P. Ananth, and
Grossenbacher.

One of the highlights for me came early in the
program. Darius read Dr. King's, "I Have a Dream"
speech. I sat there proudly as he took the podium. In the
background was video footage of Dr. King and the civil
rights movement.

After reading the speech, Darius looked down at
me. I gave him an approving nod and a smile. As I
walked to the microphone, I was pleased to see that the
banquet room was almost filled to capacity.

"Thank you all for being here tonight to honor
and celebrate Dr. King, it is my privilege to welcome you
tonight," I began. I acknowledged the support of the
mayors from the various cities and the numerous sponsors
of the event.

I read my favorite Dr. King quote, "The ultimate
measure of a man is not where he stands in times of
comfort and convenience, but where he stands in times of
challenge and controversy." The audience clapped
enthusiastically.

Ray Furstenau introduced Mr. Magwood. Upon
taking the stage Magwood acknowledged the AAA and

made a point of recognizing Darius' reading of Dr. King's speech. A special moment for our family.

Magwood's keynote address focused on the importance of education. He shared the time he visited classrooms in the Sun Valley area. He mentioned the "state of the art" computers and instruction in Sun Valley and contrasted them with the run down conditions of classrooms in Washington D.C.

He closed with, "America must do a better job providing the best education possible for all of its children."

Chapter 55 – Wow

On Wednesday, January 21, 2009 DeAnne called, "I received a voice mail from BEA's outside counsel, Larry Halvorson. He said BEA would like to attempt to negotiate a settlement. I'm more than surprised that with the decision due in 3 weeks, BEA wants to negotiate."

The fact that the offer was made just four days after the MLK banquet made me think that there was a connection.

I told DeAnne, "Maybe BEA wants to make things right, or maybe save face with DOE. Let's see what they offer." DeAnne informed Halvorson that we would entertain an offer.

On February 4, after a long day at work I returned home. As I opened the door, my phone rang.

DeAnne said, "We just received a settlement offer

from BEA, and I'm sending it via email now."

Breathlessly, I logged onto my computer and
opened the email. I was appalled. The offer was only
about a third of what we thought would be fair. Plus,
BEA would not return me to my previous position. Nor
would BEA consider a transfer to a comparable position.

The settlement offer also included a clause about
BEA not admitting any guilt. In my mind it was BEA's
last gasp effort to avoid accountability or responsibility.

The next day DeAnne sent an email to Halvorson
informing him we did not believe BEA was acting in good
faith and that we would not settle.

The morning of February 10, I awoke with great
anticipation. According to our last communication from
DOE the appeal decision would be released today. As I
left for work I told LaVonna, "Today is the day."

As the day wore on I became increasingly anxious.
By mid-afternoon I knew this would not be the day.
When I got home I collapsed onto the bed and just laid
there thinking, would this never end?

DOE had failed to issue an extension and had
communicated nothing to us about what was happening.
At the end of the week, DeAnne sent an email and
requested a status. DOE said that we should check back
at the end of the following week. This cryptic message
gave me hope that it wouldn't be much longer.

When I arrived at work on Monday morning I
passed by my old office. The door was ajar and I saw a
middle aged, heavy set gentleman sitting at the desk. He

looked up, smiled and continued unpacking boxes. The sign on the door read, "John Peterson."

Later that morning, I sent DeAnne an email asking her to send an email to DOE requesting a status report. My patience was running out and the stress was getting to me. When I came home from work I logged onto my computer to see if we heard anything from DOE. I was disappointed to see that DeAnne hadn't sent the email to DOE. I anticipated that perhaps she was reluctant to do so out of fear of annoying them.

The next day, March 10, 2009, I came home for lunch and checked my email. I had received an email from DeAnne. She told me she was reluctant to make an inquiry because the last time, DOE didn't seem too pleased and they hadn't suggested she check back. I told her I needed to hear something by the end of the week.

I laid on my bed watching TV. As the time came for me to go back to work I couldn't seem to get the energy to even get off the bed. Finally, I decided to return and try to make it through the day. As I put on my coat, my cell phone rang. My pulse quickened when I saw the phone number.

"Hi Dennis this is DeAnne." The tone of her voice told me it was good news.

"The decision just came in," I held my breath as she continued, "DOE denied BEA's appeal in its entirety."

I was speechless but managed to utter "Wow." Chills ran through my body as I realized the enormity of what this meant. DeAnne went on to say that the wording of the report was more positive than the original 2008 report.

"Thank you for believing in me and the cause I

was fighting for," I said.

"It was a pleasure," she responded. She said she
would send me the report via email as soon as we hung up.
But as fast as the internet is, I didn't have time to wait.

My first thought was that I needed to be with
LaVonna. I hurriedly put on my coat, jumped in the car
and sped down to her office. The drive to her office took
me past the INL offices. I suspected that Mark Olsen was
trying to figure out how to explain the loss to
Grossenbacher.

When I arrived at LaVonna's office, the door was
ajar so I barged in. She was standing at her desk. I had
the biggest grin on my face as I greeted her. "We won," I
declared. We grabbed each other and kissed. After nearly
four years, it was over.

LaVonna went to her computer and opened
DeAnne's email. We perused the report. It really was
better than the first one.

The following excerpt was affirming,
"Throughout its lengthy brief, BEA argues that the hearing
officer ignored, misconstrued, or inaccurately described
evidence. The hearing officer saw the witnesses testify,
listened to the tapes of the two security office interviews
of Patterson. She was thus in a position to consider the
testimony & tape recordings in conjunction with the
documentary evidence presented at the hearing. Most of
the alleged errors are mere disagreements with the hearing
officer's assessment of the testimony, evidence and
credibility of the witnesses. The hearing officer's findings
in this regard are clearly not erroneous and will be allowed
to stand. Any actual hearing officer errors are

insignificant."

It was exhilarating to read that BEA had lost on all sixty of their alleged arguments of hearing officer error.

The appeal ruling also took issue with the fact that it was the Security organization that investigated me – "Patterson's 2005 investigation found the Security office of deficiencies that resulted in corrective action. Patterson's allegations of security office and BEA management of unethical behavior led to a review of the security office by Battelle Memorial Institute."

As I had always believed, it was wrong and inappropriate for the organization I had found guilty of wrongdoing to conduct investigations of me.

After a few moments of celebrating, I told LaVonna I had to return to work to meet with my manager. Upon arriving at work, the first thing I did was send an email to friends and family. I informed everyone that I had won, again. I closed with the words "God is good."

When I arrived at Ed Anderson's office he was waiting at the doorway. He was anxious to find out the news. I had a copy of the report in my hand. I told him that DOE had issued the appeal decision, and I had won. For the next several minutes we discussed my experience being a whistleblower. Ed commented, "You know Dennis, this could be a great opportunity for BEA to learn from its mistakes and make this a better lab." I told Ed that I agreed, but it wasn't very likely. As I left his office, I told Ed I would be taking vacation for the remainder of the week.

That evening LaVonna and I celebrated at our favorite restaurant, the Sandpiper. It is where I proposed to her in 2004. Since then, it had been our favorite place.

We sat on the deck overlooking the Snake River.   The
evening was a special time of celebrating and giving
thanks.

Chapter 56 – An Illusion

March 11, 2009, the Post Register ran a story,
"DOE Whistleblower Case Closed." The headline was
quite disappointing to me for two reasons. First, the
wording did not indicate who prevailed in the case, only
that it was closed. Second, it was no longer front page
news. Only the dedicated reader would take the time to
read the article and grasp the true impact and importance
of DOE's decision.

I was outraged by BEA's response to the decision.
In 2008 Mark Olsen and Grossenbacher had sent an iNote
to all employees stating DOE was wrong and they were
appealing. This time, after losing the appeal, BEA
communicated nothing to employees.   No
acknowledgement of outcome, no acknowledgement of
wrong doing, nothing. It was as if it never happened.

A few days later, I visited with a friend in the
Internal Audit organization. I discovered that Benson had
returned to the laboratory and was now director of
"International Audits." I was shown an agenda of an
upcoming Battelle conference. The agenda included a
presentation to be conducted by Benson. The topic of the
presentation was, "Investigations and Employee
Concerns."

I couldn't believe what I was seeing. How could Battelle have Benson, a director found guilty by DOE of retaliating against the Employee Concerns Program Manager, give training to other Battelle professionals on this subject? What a sad state of affairs.

Chapter 57 – The Good and the Bad

For days, I received congratulatory emails. One email in particular caught my attention. It was sent by a prominent community leader, Sheila Olsen. She and I shared a close friend, Americus John-Lewis (AJ). Sheila sent me the following message, "Congratulations Dennis! What a wonderful example of faith, courage, perseverance, patience, and standing for right this is! I am so happy for you and so proud to call you my friend."

AJ, a devout Roman Catholic and Sheila, a devout member of the LDS church, years earlier had put together a 24 hour multidenominational prayer-a-thon. To be congratulated and recognized by Sheila was quite special. I suspected that AJ was looking down from heaven with a smile.

My pastor wrote, "This has been a long hard struggle, but through the process you have blessed others along the journey in ways you can't imagine." These words of inspiration from the leader of my spiritual life were very humbling. Other messages received included:

"This is great news it gives hope to all that we do."

"I am glad justice was finally served."

"You and your family have been in our thoughts and prayers I did so pray for this to happen."

"Praise the Lord (several emails contained this message)"

"Halleluiah!!" (one of my favorites)

Every morning when I woke up it was easier to get out of bed. Taking a shower was more pleasurable, the coffee tasted better and the sun seemed to shine brighter. Life was good!

A few days after I won the appeal, I stopped by my office to see if I had any email or phone messages. I opened my email and saw a meeting invite from Grossenbacher. The invitation simply said, "Discussion with Dennis Patterson."

Finally, after almost four years, I was getting the opportunity to meet with him. The good feeling lasted only seconds. I noticed that Grossenbacher had also invited Mark Olsen to the meeting.

Back in 2005, when I told Olsen I wanted a meeting with Grossenbacher, he tried to intimidate me by barking, "do you really want to take me on." Olsen had been part of the ongoing harassment and retaliation. I accepted the meeting invitation but requested that Olsen not attend and explained my reasons. I told Grossenbacher, if a senior manager needed to be present, I recommended Dr. Harold Blackman.

Approximately a week later Grossenbacher wrote back and informed me Olsen would not be attending. The meeting was scheduled for April 3, 2009.

171

As the meeting day approached my feelings fluctuated between excitement and anticipation to dread and anxiety. The morning of the meeting I read scriptures, prayed and took notes of what I wanted to say. As I entered Grossenbacher's office, I was saw Harold Blackman. Grossenbacher met me at the door and shook my hand. As we sat at the table the tension was palpable.

John began, "Dennis you are a valued employee. I wanted to give you a chance to meet with me. The whistleblower case is over. I want our conversation to focus on the future. What do you have to say?"

I thanked him and began, "John as a long time employee and a native of Idaho Falls I am committed to the success of the laboratory. I filed the whistleblower complaint because I believed that in the end it would help make the INL a better place to work. We have to create a work environment where employees feel valued and respected."

We discussed issues including safety, pension plan, diversity, retention, attrition and senior leadership. After about 45 minutes, John closed his folder and moved away from the table as though to say the meeting was over. For me, the meeting wasn't over. John had said nothing about my career.

The DOE report issued on March 9, 2009 recommended that BEA consider reinstating me to the Ethics Officer/Employee Concerns position. It also directed, as an alternative, for BEA to identify a "comparable position." As John rose to leave, he asked, "is there anything else.' I'm sure he expected me to say no. Of course, since he invited me to talk, I would talk. I was not going to rely on bureaucracy and legal maneuvering to determine my future. This time, it was going to be Grossenbacher and Patterson, face to face.

"Yes John, there is something else. I would like to talk about my career." I watched his face as I asked the question. He couldn't have been more stoic. It was as if he was void of feelings or emotion.

"You are just like any other employee, if you see a job opening apply for it, if you get it great, if not keep trying," he said. I was stunned by his response. The idea that he would say I was just like any other employee was very hurtful. BEA had intimidated, harassed and taken retribution against me. I had been investigated multiple times, unfairly escorted from the premises of the INL, and removed from the job I loved.

I took a deep breath and replied, "John, we seem to have a different understanding of the DOE report. I believe that BEA has a responsibility to find me a comparable job." Again, his face showed no sign of emotion.

"Have you read the DOE report?" I asked.

"I haven't read it in detail, but I will and then we'll meet again. You may not like what I say, but we'll talk again."

He quickly retracted the latter remark and said, "Well, let's just say I'll give you a response." He asked, "Is that fair?"

"Yes," was all I could say.

We stood and shook hands. I looked at Harold, who had remained silent throughout the meeting. As we exited, Harold asked how I was doing. I said, "Fine." Of course, I wasn't fine, and I'm sure he knew it. I hadn't

DENNIS PATTERSON

expected an apology but I didn't expect Grossenbacher to
act as though nothing had happened.

I had been in regular communications with
DeAnne. She had been speaking with Larry Halvorson
about the details of the decision and trying to reach final
resolution. The major sticking point appeared to be
DOE's recommendation that BEA consider placing me
back in the Ethics/Employee Concerns office or finding a
comparable position. Of course, every action taken by
BEA over the past four years indicated that they would
never do this. We soon learned that BEA legal had
informed DOE OHA that they would not reinstate me
and that they would not find another position for me.
They argued, and convinced DOE OHA, that my current
position in engineering was 'comparable" and therefore no
further action was necessary. They also argued that they
had already hired someone to fill the position and it would
create a hardship on him.

I was outraged, not just at BEA but also the DOE
Office of Hearings and Appeals. I considered writing
directly to the DOE Energy Secretary, Dr. Steven Chu.
Not putting me back in the office or finding a comparable
job was not only unfair but wholly inconsistent with
providing protections to whistleblowers.

Another point of contention arose when Mark Olsen
and Katherine Moriarty sent me an email informing me
that BEA would not remove my unfair 2006 performance
appraisal from my personnel file. How could they refuse
to follow a direct order from the hearing officer?

I decided to send an email to Juan Alvarez asking him
to intervene. Within 24 hours the appraisal was removed
from my file. I was amazed. A BEA senior manager had
made the right decision and it didn't take forever to do so.

A rewarding moment and great relief came near the end of the process. I went down to DeAnne's office to take care of a little paperwork. BEA had submitted the check to pay my attorney fees. The check was in excess of eighty thousand dollars. As I signed the check over to Holden, Hahn, Kidwell and Crapo, the relief was as much physical as it was mental and emotional. I hadn't fully appreciated how heavy the financial burden had been. But now, this part was over. No more worries about losing the house or paying for the kid's college education.

Chapter 58 – Ghost from the Past

A few days after my meeting with Grossenbacher I received an email from Juan Alvarez, Deputy Laboratory Director for Management. He and Mark Holubar, Human Resource director, wanted to meet with me to discuss my future. This gave me a sense of hope and excitement. Of course, the good feeling was tempered by the fact that Alvarez had written the letter in 2005 that questioned my fitness to be Ethics Officer/Employee Concerns Manager.

I entered Alvarez's office. Juan greeted me with a smile and a handshake.

"I've read the DOE report and I believe this is the right thing to do. We are not doing this because we have to, we are doing it because we believe it is best for everyone," Juan said.

Holubar said BEA wanted to create a job that would leverage my skills, experience, and abilities. At the end of the meeting, Holubar mentioned a personality profile questionnaire, "Dennis, we want you to take the Hogan Assessment."

I immediately became suspicious, and asked, "How many BEA employees have taken this assessment?"

"None," Holubar replied.

"Well, I'm not comfortable being the first, especially under the circumstances," I replied.

Alvarez interrupted, "Dennis, take a couple of days and think about it."

Later that evening, LaVonna and I discussed whether I should take the assessment as requested. Although wary, we decided that building trust had to start somewhere. The next time I met with Juan and Mark I told them I would take the assessment. The following week I completed the several page questionnaire. The subject areas included business philosophy, leadership style, personal attributes and ethics. A few days after completing the assessment I spent three hours on the phone with a Battelle corporate officer reviewing the results. Overall, I was very pleased with the results, as was the corporate person. The report identified "ethics" as an area of strength for me.

Two weeks later I again met with Juan and Mark. This time they had a formal position description and offered me the job. I would report directly to Juan with responsibility for developing a manager workshop and leading a new laboratory initiative to measure and improve employee engagement. The job required regular interface and coordination with senior leadership.

Juan committed to provide a private office for me, comparable to the one I had as Ethics Officer. Juan gave

me a copy of the job description and asked me to let him
know if I would accept within a couple days.

On the surface this appeared to be a great opportunity.
I had one serious reservation. One thing was an almost a
certainty. If budgets became tight, this would become
one of the first positions to be eliminated. Additionally,
being a whistleblower put a target on my back. It was
unlikely I could find another job here at the lab or
anywhere in Battelle or DOE.

After much prayer, LaVonna and I agreed that I
really didn't have much choice. I started two weeks later.

I readily acclimated myself to the new job and new
surroundings. One of the first things I did was look up
the organizational chart for Alvarez. Turned out, Juan
only had eight employees in his organization. One of
them was Doug Benson, my arch enemy for the past four
years. Another was the former state legislator who was
accused of conducting political activity using government
equipment. I chuckled when I saw the two names and
wondered what it would be like to attend staff meetings. It
also gave me a bit of pause, as I considered the possibility
that Juan's organization was the place where "misfits"
came to finish off their careers.

Chapter 59 – The Summit

In the spring of 2009 Ed Turner, city of Idaho Falls whistleblower, contacted me and suggested that we convene a "Whistleblower Summit" – a gathering of whistleblowers. Ed told me that he knew Roger Boisjoly, the lead engineer for the Challenger Space Shuttle. We decided to invite Roger as our special guest.

The Summit was convened at the Red Lion Hotel in Pocatello, Idaho. Other attendees included two former INL whistleblowers, Darryl Siemer and Ben Cowan. Because our spouses were part of the whistleblower experience they were invited as well.

The conference room was small with a rectangular table in the middle. Ed led the introductions and explained that we were here to share our stories, and explore ways in which we could support each other and other whistleblowers. Each whistleblower told his story. Everyone's experience, except mine, had happened more than ten years ago. Yet, they could cite details as if it had been yesterday. The most compelling part of each story was the personal journey and how they had survived and in some cases thrived.

The highlight of the whistleblower summit was hearing from Roger. We asked him to share his story at the end so that he would have as much time as needed. Roger began by showing us a model of "O-rings" of the typed that failed in the January 28, 1986 Challenger disaster. It was kind of eerie just looking at them. Roger explained the scientific and technical nature of the O-ring failure, but more importantly he shared his personal story.

With pain on his face, Roger described being part of the teleconference between Thiokol and the Kennedy Space Center the night before the launch. He spoke of

presenting information that described major concerns with
the resiliency of the O rings under low temperatures.
Thiokol had ended the presentation with the
recommendation not to launch the next day. Roger noted
that it was clear NASA was unhappy with the "no launch"
recommendation.

Roger said he participated in the subsequent Thiokol
discussions about what to do. The discussions were tense
and heated as Roger and his team continued to argue
against launching the next day. Roger related that at one
point a senior Thiokol manager said, "Take off your
engineering hat and put on your management hat." In the
end, in spite of Roger's efforts, Thiokol senior
management gave NASA the recommendation to launch.
Roger watched the launch while sitting on the floor of the
viewing room. Seconds later the Challenger exploded,
killing all seven crew members.

"The horror was overwhelming, I went back to my
office and remained there, alone for the rest of the day,"
he explained.

As we went around the room each spouse shared her
story. When it came to Mrs. Boisjoly, she quietly said,
"I'm sorry, but it is still too painful." The look on her face
told us all we needed to know.

After the meeting, LaVonna and I had a chance to
visit with Roger and Roberta. Roberta spoke of the
heartbreaking experience of watching her husband go
through the emotional and psychological pain of being
punished and persecuted by his company for testifying
truthfully during the congressional hearings and
investigations. Colleagues, friends, and members of their

small community often shunned him.

As we said goodbye, LaVonna and I expressed our admiration and respect for both of them. Roberta responded, "We are proud of you both, and will keep you in our prayers." As we left the whistleblower summit I felt honored and privileged to have met Roger and Roberta Boisjoly.

Chapter 60 – Success

The summer of 2009 was relaxing and exciting. The relief could be felt every night when I went to sleep and every morning when I awoke. The excitement of a job that I enjoyed, sometimes felt too good to be true.

One of my primary job duties was leading a new BEA initiative. BEA had recently decided to contract with the Gallup Corporation to conduct annual all employee surveys. The purpose was to measure "employee engagement." Engagement surveys measured the employees' emotional and psychological commitment to the company. I found it quite ironic that a former whistleblower would be leading this effort.

During the month of July, approximately 80% of all employees voluntarily participated in the anonymous survey. Senior management was anxious to get the results. They did not expect very good results. In September, Gallup sent us the survey results. The overall score placed BEA in the bottom 15% when compared to other national laboratories. In many ways, I felt vindicated. The results let me know I was not alone in my views of the work environment.

Managers were required to share their organizational
results with their employees and collaborate with
employees to identify actions to improve the work
environment in their work group. I led a team of
employees responsible for providing direction and
oversight of the program.

In September, Juan asked me to host an on-line
discussion (blog) of employee engagement. Just a few
months removed from being a whistleblower, and now I
was hosting a discussion about the lab with all employees.
Over the next year, I facilitated meetings, shared best
practices, tracked progress, and made recommendations to
management.

In late fall, I heard rumors that Mark Olsen was
leaving the laboratory. This didn't surprise me. Olsen had
been the primary person responsible for the failed defense
of my whistleblower complaint. I hoped the rumors of his
departure were true. It would be best for BEA and best
for BEA employees.

My other main job assignment was development of a
management workshop called "Mandate to Manage." The
workshop included the key operational areas of the lab
including finance, legal, safety, human resources, audit, and
the four mission areas.

Each module was taught by the senior manager of
each function. The pilot was successfully launched in
February 2010. It signaled a successful beginning to my
new career at the INL.

Chapter 61 – "Learning, Earning, Returning"

As winter approached, I was busy helping to plan the 2010 Dr. King banquet. The AAA decided to invite Dr. Pete Miller to be the keynote speaker. Miller had just been nominated by President Obama to be Director of Nuclear Energy for the Department of Energy. Miller was confirmed, and became the person responsible for oversight and management of the INL.

There were some who believed we had zero chance of getting an acceptance because it was the dead of winter in Idaho. Surely, Miller would have more enticing speaking opportunities. Nonetheless, we prepared an invitation letter. I sent it via email from my office at 11:25 a.m. and then left to meet LaVonna for lunch. At 11:43 a.m. my blackberry beeped. I opened up my email and was please to read, "I would be honored to speak at your event."

The banquet was held on Friday, January 15. Seated at the head table was Dr. Miller; Michelle Scott, his assistant; John Grossenbacher and his wife Kathy; Dennis Miotla, acting DOE-ID manager; and LaVonna and myself. LaVonna looked stunning in her new green dress. After Dr. Miller recognized distinguished guests he commented, "Dennis Patterson has become a new friend and so has his lovely wife." This was a proud moment for me.

During Dr. Miller's keynote address we learned that as a child one of his good friends was Emmett Till. That fateful summer in 1955, Pete Miller, 14 years old, was living in Chicago. Emmett's family had invited Pete to go with them on a family vacation to Mississippi. Pete's mother, aware of the dangers of the south, refused to let Pete go with his friend, the same age as Pete. History tells us the rest of the story. While in Mississippi, two white men beat Emmett and dumped his body in the

Tallahatchie River with a cotton gin fan tied around his
neck with barbed wire. The audience gasped upon hearing
a story that until now was just words in a history book.

Miller closed with, "I would like to leave you with
advice I learned from my father a long time ago. You
should spend your life, one third learning, one third
earning and one third returning." Weeks after the
banquet folks were still talking about Dr. Miller's talk and
the profound impact it had on them.

Chapter 62 – An Apology and a Trip

One morning, shortly after arriving at work I received
a call from Juan's administrator. She told me Juan wanted
to meet with me right away. Not knowing why I was
summoned caused a bit of anxiety.

Juan greeted me and closed the door, "Dennis, I
would like you to go to Washington D.C for a two week
assignment."

"I would love to" I said, before even knowing the
details.

"This is a professional development opportunity, it
will benefit you as well as the laboratory," Juan said.

I would attend congressional budget hearings and have the opportunity to attend meetings with Idaho congressional representatives including Mike Simpson and Mike Crapo. Juan also arranged for me to meet senior Battelle executives and senior DOE personnel. Juan added, "It will also be a great opportunity for you to visit with Pete Miller." I had the feeling that BEA was trying to leverage my relationship with Dr. Miller,

As the meeting came to a close, Juan shifted in his chair. Almost painfully, he brought up the subject of my whistleblower complaint.

"Dennis, I regret sending the letter to Benson back when all this started," he said.

I almost fell out of my chair.

He continued, "If I had a problem with you I should have invited you to my office and talked to you. Maybe we could have worked it through and avoided all of this."

"Yes, that would have been better. The letter damaged my reputation and it felt like retaliation. Why didn't you talk to me later on?" I asked.

"Because Olsen advised me to have no communications with you," he answered. Juan added, "If there is one lesson I have learned, it's that a company should never forget that the employee is still a person, not just a whistleblower."

I realized that this was the closest thing to an apology that I would ever get. Finally, a BEA senior manager had acknowledged some accountability.

On March 22nd I found myself on a plane to Washington D.C. Almost exactly a year ago I had won my whistleblower complaint. For two weeks, I stayed at the

W Hotel, across the street from the White House. I
attended hearings, breakfast meetings and met senior
DOE and Battelle managers. I was tempted to stop by the
office of Hearing Officer, Adeyeye, but decided against it.
I wasn't sure of the protocol, but I'm sure she would have
enjoyed hearing "the rest of the story."

On my last day in D. C. I decided to walk the halls of
Congress. During my walk I noticed an office with the
name "Representative John Lewis, Georgia." I had long
admired and respected John Lewis. I remembered him
marching with Dr. King and being arrested and jailed
many times.

I entered the reception area and introduced myself. I
asked if there was any possibility of shaking Congressman
Lewis's hand. I was told yes and to have a seat.

A few minutes later he came out, smiled and extended
his hand, "Good afternoon, welcome, please come into my
office."

His office was large and spacious, befitting someone
who had served his country for so many years. The room
was filled with historical documents, newspapers, and
pictures that told of the civil rights struggle. There was a
picture of the August 28, 1963 March on Washington.
John told me that he had given a speech that day as the
chair of the Student Nonviolent Coordinating Committee,
prior to Dr. King's speech. He told of how he cried the
day that Dr. King was assassinated.

"King taught all of us how to speak up and speak out
whenever there is injustice," he said.

I responded: "Dr. King has been my hero since I was

185

a little boy. A few years ago, I helped organize a community non-profit, the African American Alliance. Each year we honor Dr. King with a banquet in Idaho Falls."

"Tell your organization thank you for what it is doing," he responded.

At the end of our visit he summoned a staffer to take our picture shaking hands on the balcony of his office, with the U.S Capitol in the background.

"Thank you for your courage and sacrifice for our country," I said.

As I walked out of his office I wasn't sure my feet were touching the ground. I felt as though I had just journeyed with Dr. King.

On my way out I took the elevator. I glanced around and was surprised to see Congresswoman Debbie Wasserman Schultz. I decided that I would get off with her and introduce myself. She politely shook my hand and told me she enjoyed working with Idaho's congressional delegation. This was a fitting end to a wonderful day.

Chapter 63 – Homeland Security

In February 2012 several employees from the National Homeland Security organization stopped by my cubicle. They told me that a manager in their organization had filed a whistleblower complaint with the Department of Energy. The person that filed the complaint was a former highly decorated Navy SEAL who served 30 years, including 15 years with the SEAL team that killed Osama

Bin Laden.

I informed the employees that if a whistleblower complaint had indeed been filed, DOE would post the results on the Office of Hearings and Appeals web site. Each of the employees said that they were certain that the complaint was filed and most said they believed there was merit to the allegation. They described what they believed was an intimidating and hostile work environment where employees were punished for speaking up. They told me that the DOE-Idaho Employee Concerns office had investigated some of the issues and concluded that management's actions had created a "chilling effect" i.e. employees were afraid to raise issues or report misconduct.

Chapter 64 – Farewell and You're Fired

On March 4, 2010 an iNote was sent to all employees, "We bid farewell to Mark Olsen, Effective April 19 he will become associate general counsel – Laboratory Operations for Battelle Memorial Institute in Columbus, Ohio. His primary responsibility will be to perform/oversee the legal work for Battelle's Laboratory Operations Organization which oversees six DOE national laboratories, the National Biodefense Analysis and Countermeasures Center, and National Nuclear Laboratory in the United Kingdom. A special thanks goes to Mark for his contributions as general counsel since the creation of the new INL."

Like Benson, Olsen was being transfered to Battelle corporate with an apparent promotion. I guessed this was the "BEA Way." You screw up enough and they send you to corporate with a nice farewell iNote message.

On October 5, 2010, I was sitting at my desk when I noticed a special iNote announcement from Grossenbacher, "I regret to announce that I have directed Dwayne Coburn to turn over his duties as Facilities and Site Services director and acting director for the Project Management office by the end of this week, and thus he will no longer be employed at Idaho National Laboratory. This action is a result of failure to achieve leadership and standards that are an expectation of leaders and managers at INL."

I sat and stared at my computer screen for several minutes. Never before had an INL President publically announced the removal of a senior manager. Yet, Grossenbacher just did it.

BEA wasn't as honest and forthright when Benson and Olsen were reassigned. In my opinion the only reason Coburn received such treatment was because, according to rumor, this was at least the third time he had a relationship with a subordinate.

According to credible sources, Coburn was not the only senior BEA manager with a history of inappropriate relationships. At least two other senior managers were widely rumored to be engaged in similar practices. In fact, I brought one of the managers to the attention of a Deputy Laboratory Director, who said, "I know but since we don't have a 'smoking gun,' there's nothing we can do."

In my mind this was wrong. BEA didn't need a "smoking gun" to discipline me or to ruin the careers of other employees. Obviously senior managers were held to a different standard and that standard wasn't very high. The real tragedy of this story is that the trust and integrity of BEA had been damaged over the past few years.

Many employees were long aware that Coburn had
inappropriate relationships with subordinate staff
members. He had been previously warned by
Grossenbacher about such behavior. BEA implemented a
specific policy that required employees (managers and
employees) to fill out a disclosure form if a romantic
relationship existed. When the policy was issued it was
joked about, and sometimes referred to as the "Coburn
Affair" policy.

To me, the issuance of a policy was ridiculous and
ineffective. The more appropriate action would have been
to discipline Coburn the first time. Most employees
believed that Grossenbacher was a person of integrity, but
his failure to adequately address management misconduct
stained his reputation and the company's.

I was hopeful that this iNote signaled a positive
change in how BEA would address management
misconduct in the future. Little did I realize that a couple
years in the future this iNote would once again be the talk
of the laboratory, but for a reason that no one could have
predicted.

Chapter 65 – An Eventful 2010

After a year of working to improve the work
environment BEA senior management was optimistic
that the results from the 2010 Gallup survey would be
more positive. The results were released in October.

The improvement was significant. INL had gone from being in the bottom 15% compared to other labs to the 35th percentile. According to Gallup, this was one of the largest one year increases they had seen for a large institution like the INL.

When we communicated the results lab-wide there was significant skepticism amongst the troops. Some employees questioned the validity of the survey and others refused to believe that the improvement was real. Much of the skepticism was due to BEA's efforts over the past year to eliminate the early retirement portion of the INL pension plan. This issue had been a major source of concern, some might say outrage, within the work place.

Many long time employees felt betrayed by the company and felt that such an action was unethical if not illegal. Employees had openly complained to senior BEA management to no avail. Some employees had taken the issue to the local press, DOE-Idaho, and even the Idaho congressional delegation.

One day I noticed an official looking letter hanging on the wall in the men's restroom. The letterhead read, "Congress of the United States House of Representatives." The letter was addressed to Mr. Pete Miller, Assistant Secretary, Office of Nuclear Energy. The letter dated June 29, 2010, was from Idaho Congressman Mike Simpson, "I am writing today to express my opposition to the plan proposed by the Idaho National Laboratory (INL) to alter the early retirement portion of its pension plan system in an effort to update employee benefits. As you know, this proposal has generated considerable interest among my constituents and many INL employees. In particular, I am concerned that, in order to help offset the cost of new benefits for younger employees, the

most loyal, long-term members of INL's workforce
will see what I consider to be unfair reductions in their
early retirement benefits. In closing, it is important to
remember that numbers and headcounts do not always
determine the difference between right and wrong,
and numbers alone cannot justify an action that is
inequitable and unjust. I appreciate the motivation for
improving the front-end benefits INL offers to new or
prospective employees, but I cannot support the
deterioration of benefits for existing employees that
this proposal requires."

This was a great example of how the American
political and representative process should work.
Citizens must have an avenue to protect their interests
because corporate interests are often quite different.

On November 3, 2010 a Special iNote message
from Grossenbacher was released, "I have decided to
withdraw our request to DOE to make changes to the
defined benefit plan and defined contribution 401k
plan. Since submission of the request it has
undergone several adjustments. Additionally it is no
longer economically viable..."

This was a tribute to BEA employees and to
Congressman Simpson. The employees who had
dedicated their lives to the INL would not have their
pension cut.

At the end of the year, several employees told me that
the whistleblower from the National Homeland
Security (NHS) organization had lost his case. I
logged onto the internet and discovered that they were
correct. DOE had ruled in favor of BEA.

This former Navy Seal, turned whistleblower, was terminated in 2011. After his termination the new General Counsel and the Human Resource director conducted meetings with NHS employees. They told employees that his firing was justified and totally unrelated to his being a whistleblower. After these meetings, several employees stopped by my cubicle to visit. Most believed the meetings were a farce and that they were only held to protect the interests of BEA.

According to sources, the person later filed a civil lawsuit against BEA and settled out of court for an undisclosed amount of money. Rumor was that the person likely wouldn't have to work for a long time.

I later spoke with the DOE Idaho Employee Concerns Manager about this case and the actions of BEA senior management. Following the discussion, she mentioned that there was something she had wanted to tell me for a long time.

"Dennis, I wish I had been of more help to you. I should have never allowed BEA to attempt to force you to disclose the confidential source. I wanted BEA to reinstate you as the Ethics and Employee Concerns Manager."

She also expressed displeasure with how BEA has operated the Employee Concerns program since I was removed. She said that the office no longer has the appropriate level of independence and neutrality.

"I believe that is how BEA wants it," she said.

2010 had been a very good year for me. Early in the year, LaVonna and I had joined another small group at church. On Saturday mornings we met at a

local coffee shop and discussed inspirational Christian
books. No matter the situation or circumstance,
LaVonna and I always left the bistro feeling blessed
and encouraged by our dear friends.

Professionally, this was the first year since 2004
that I wasn't in the midst of challenge and
controversy. In my annual performance review with
Alvarez I received praise and recognition for my
contributions to the success of the INL. As I
prepared to leave his office he handed me an envelope
and said "job well done." I waited until I returned to
my office to open it. Inside was a commendation
letter with a personal note of appreciation, along with
a check. Yes indeed, it had been a very good year!

Chapter 66 – 2011 Dr. King Banquet

It was now time for the 2011 Dr. Martin Luther
King banquet. This year we were fortunate to have a
very special keynote speaker, Dr. Debbie Thomas. At
this point, I was no longer president of the African
American Alliance. After the 2010 banquet I had
decided it was time to step down. My good friend
David Snell, assumed the presidency.

Prior to the banquet Debbie held an autograph
session at the local hockey shelter. It was a pleasure
watching her visit with the youth as she signed
autographs and posed for pictures. Many of these
same kids came to the banquet.

In her keynote address, Debbie spoke about being a young child with a dream of becoming a champion figure skater and a doctor and how she had succeeded at both. She won the World Figure Skating Championship and was the first African American to win a medal in Winter Olympics, winning the bronze medal in figure staking at the 1988 winter Olympics. She got her medical degree in 1997 and served her residence at the Martin Luther King/Charles Drew University Medical Center in South Central Los Angeles.

Dr. Thomas' message was inspiring to young and old alike.

Chapter 67 – Tragic Events

In early June 2011 several colleagues stopped by my cubicle to visit about the latest happenings at the INL. They told me there had been a serious and potentially catastrophic event at the Advanced Test Reactor. They said that the water level in the nuclear reactor had drained down to about half. A troubling part of this situation was that nothing was being communicated about this event. Days, weeks and months passed with no word from the company. Employees, including myself, were distressed that BEA was apparently choosing to withhold information from employees, and the community, about such a critical event.

On November 9, 2011 there was another major event, but this time with tragic consequences. The Post Register ran the following front page headline,

"Workers Exposed at INL." The following excerpts
were in the article:

"At least six workers were exposed to plutonium
radiation from a container opened Tuesday at the
Idaho National Laboratory site's Material & Fuel
Complex."

"As of 10:30 p.m., about 9.5 hours after the
exposure was reported, few details about the source
and severity of the incident were known. A team of
INL specialists agreed that radiation was contained
within the building where the exposure occurred and
that the public and environment were not at risk."

"A total of 17 workers who were in the proximity
of the exposure when it occurred underwent initial
decontamination, according to an INL statement. The
measures taken during initial decontamination were
unclear."

"The workers then were taken to the INL site's
medical facility for full body scans. Six of them were
determined to have received external contamination to
the skin or clothing."

"As of Tuesday night, no internal contamination
had been discovered. Nonetheless all 17 workers
accepted precautionary internal treatments designed to
remove plutonium that they may have inhaled or
swallowed, Lab spokesman Ethan Huffman said."

"It's unclear why opening the container caused a
release of plutonium or why workers were not using
equipment to shield them from the plutonium."

"This is at least the second time since 2010 that a worker has been exposed to radiation at the Materials and Fuels Complex. Last year a worker nearly exceeded his yearly allowed radiation dose because lab officials underestimated the amount of radiation exposure he would face in his duties." (Reporter, Sven Berg)

As I read the story I had no idea that one day I would be sitting across the table from one of the impacted employees. And that this person would himself become a whistleblower.

Chapter 68 – Trying to Make a Difference

In November 2011, I was watching the news one evening and saw something that caught my attention. There were allegations of child molestation at Penn State University (PSU). During the news broadcasts it was announced that PSU would soon be hiring an Ethics Officer.

A couple of days later I sent an email to the president of PSU. I received a response the same day. The email was from the Vice President. He thanked me for my interest in the ethics officer position and noted that he would forward my correspondence to the appropriate person. Although I knew that it was unlikely anything would come of my inquiry, it felt good knowing that I had tried.

In my email, I mentioned my whistleblower case and said that whomever they select must have the courage and conviction to protect the rights, safety and health of others, even at the sacrifice of self.

During an exchange of text messages with Darius
I shared with him my communications with PSU. The
following day I was filled with pride when I read a
Facebook post by Darius, "I hope that one day I will
be a positive impact in people's lives and accomplish
as much as my father has." I responded, "Hey son, I
believe you are already on your way – it begins with
the desire to make a difference. I am proud to call you
my son. "

By the end of 2011, I was feeling good about my
job and looked forward to continuing my career at the
INL. LaVonna's counseling and psychology practice
was going well and we were enjoying life.

Chapter 69 – "You Have a Charge to Keep"

The 2012 Dr. King banquet featured Bruce
Smith as the keynote speaker. Bruce was a senior
animator for Disney films. He had supervised
animation on Tarzan, The Emperor's New Groove,
Princess and the Frog, and Winnie the Pooh.

He was also the creator and producer of the
Proud Family, a Disney animated TV sitcom about a
14 year old African American girl and her family.
Bruce was a very engaging and entertaining speaker.
He shared his personal story of trials, tribulations and
successes, as a trailblazer in the animated film industry.
He spoke about the need for greater diversity and how
he used people from his life experience in characters
he had animated. He encouraged the children to

pursue their dreams with hard work and determination. He closed with, "Thank you Idaho Falls for bringing me out here, this is a beautiful place. We are all family, young and old." The crowd was delighted by his inspiring and hopeful keynote presentation.

Also on the program was the honorable Cherie Buckner-Webb, Idaho's first African American state legislator, and co-founder of Idaho's Black History Museum in Boise, ID. During her remarks she told the audience, "You have a charge to keep." She explained that this was an old time phrase that means we still have work to do. She added, "If anyone lives in injustice we all live in injustice." Cherie added to the evening's enjoyment with a beautiful rendition of, "He Looked Beyond My Faults."

The banquet was a great success. The African American Alliance was privileged to present a check for $2,500 to a local non-profit, HELP Inc., an organization committed to fighting child abuse and assisting families in crisis.

Chapter 70 – Now we Know

On February 8, 2012 there was an article in the Post Register, "The United States DOE fined the contractor that runs INL $250,000 for a June 2011incident at the Advanced Test Reactor. In the incident, which took place during a scheduled maintenance shutdown, about half of the reactors coolant was drained accidentally from the reactor vessel, a problem that operators did not notice for

more than 2 hours, according to a DOE document.
Draining the coolant did not result in any adverse
effects on the worker, public or (reactor) systems, said
a letter from DOE to INL director John
Grossenbacher, 'Nevertheless DOE considers this
event to be of high nuclear safety significance'."
(Reporter, Sven Berg)

The following day February 9, 2012, BEA sent
an iNote to employees. The iNote referred to the
Post Register story, and included the following, "The
details of the ATR incident were discussed by INL
Lab Director John Grossenbacher in the most recent
all-employee meetings (see link below)."

I couldn't believe what I was reading. I had
attended the employee meetings in October 2011.
Grossenbacher did not provide any details. If fact, he
barely mentioned what happened. I clicked on the
link in the iNote. The link contained a video
recording of one of Grossenbacher's all employee
meetings.

Approximately mid-way into the video there was
a slide titled, "Operational Performance" with the
following bulleted item:

- "ATR corrective actions from the inadvertent
  vessel draining process."
  I replayed the video several times in an
  effort to capture Grossenbacher's comments.
  This is what I heard him say, "Of course, this is
  for our performance problems both at MFC and
  ATR, Radcon and work control at ATR and water

level control. We got the right people doing the right thing to improve our performance."

Grossenbacher did not share details as stated in the iNote. He never mentioned that the water in the reactor continued to drain for two hours. He didn't tell employees that the reactor lost half of the water. He didn't tell us that DOE was conducting an investigation that could lead to substantial fines and penalties.

Seven months after an operational event "of high nuclear safety significance" and this was the first time BEA had sent out an iNote to employees. And then, the iNote contained misleading information. BEA had the audacity and arrogance to include a "link" that was supposed to make the untruth seem true. Apparently BEA was betting that no one would actually click on the link. I was disgusted with how BEA had handled this matter. Many of my colleagues and friends expressed similar feelings. A couple of folks told me they were afraid for the safety and health of employees. Their fear – "that someone might get killed."

Chapter 71 – My Career

Late in February 2012, I met with Juan to discuss my performance for 2011 and my goals and objectives for 2012.

Juan began, "your performance for 2011 met all of my expectations." He then added, "Dennis you have the right skills and abilities to

do well in the Labor Relations organization. I
would like you to spend at least two months
working in labor relations. I want you to learn the
function and operations of the organization. This
may be a viable career path for you."

I didn't know for sure, but I sensed that
the unspoken message was that my current job
was in jeopardy and Juan was looking for a way to
move me to another organization.

I responded, "I look forward to the
opportunity and the challenge." Juan said he
would set up a meeting with the Labor Relations
manager, Mark Wangler to make this happen.

On March 25, 2012 Juan and I met
with Wangler. During the forty minute meeting,
for 35 minutes Wangler talked about his own
successes and triumphs in the labor relations
world. In the final five minutes, Juan explained to
Wangler his intention to have me spend time in
his organization.

"Sure Juan, we can make this happen.
Dennis contact me next week and we'll get
together," Wangler said.

The next week I sent Wangler an email
referencing our meeting with Juan and my
availability to meet any time. I heard nothing
from Wangler over the next two weeks. I sent
him a reminder on April 30. Again, I heard
nothing. On May 14, I sent another email. Still
no response. I concluded that Wangler had no
intention of meeting with me.

I suspected that Wangler had found out I was a whistleblower. He likely decided it would be best to have nothing to do with me. He may have even felt like Juan was trying to pull one over on him. Of course, all of this was just conjecture on my part. The only thing I knew for certain was that after repeated attempts to communicate with him, I didn't even receive the courtesy of a "thanks but no thanks."

After not hearing from Wangler for several weeks I contacted his boss, Director of Human Resources, Mark Holubar. Holubar said he didn't know anything about this, but would follow-up and get back to me.

By now, it was clear BEA had no interest in furthering my career. So, I chose to make the best of a difficult situation. A year ago, the INL decided to sponsor the first ever INL Toastmaster club. I had joined, hopeful that one day I could begin a new career giving speeches to inspire and motivate others.

On May 12, 2012, The Toastmasters District 15 speech contest was held in Salt Lake City. I participated in the "Table Topics" category. This competition tests a person's ability to give a short speech, on the spot, without any preparation. When my turn came I was introduced and given the question, "If you could interview anyone past or present, who would it be and what would you ask?" Without pausing, I said that it would be Dr. Martin Luther King Jr. Instinctively, I reflected back to 2006 when I participated on a diversity panel in Idaho Falls. After the panel discussion, I was asked my opinion on whether Dr. King would support the right of gays to be married.

"Dr. King would oppose gay marriage because he

was a minister and the bible teaches that homosexuality is
a sin," is how I responded in 2006.

But today I no longer believed this. Here in the
midst of perhaps the most conservative city in America I
responded.

"I believe that Dr. King would support gay
marriage, because it is a matter of equality and fairness."

I knew that saying so could jeopardize my chance
to win the competition, but I plunged ahead. As I spoke I
looked in the eyes of the audience members. To my
surprise, I could see compassion and understanding.

I was chosen as the first place winner. As I
accepted the trophy, I felt proud to have stood on
principle rather than convenience. Jasmine gave me a big
smile and said she was proud of me. Later she told me she
had gotten a new tattoo. It was a quote from Maya
Angelou, "In diversity there is beauty and strength."

On July 18, 2012, there was a special INL
ceremony in honor of a friend, Mary Dee Grimm.
She had just reached her 50 year anniversary with
the INL and it was my privilege to attend the
celebration. Mary Dee represented the best of the
INL – outstanding work ethic, honesty, integrity
and highly respected by colleagues and staff.

Holubar was present at the ceremony, but
for most of the event he avoided me. When I
finally got his attention, before even saying hello,
he said, "Hey Dennis, I talked to Wangler, he said
he would have to get back to me." By this time I
was convinced this whole thing was a farce. There

was going to be no professional development opportunity as Juan had suggested.

"No problem Mark, just let me know," I said with resignation. The lack of integrity was disheartening but no longer a surprise.

Later in August, I met with Juan.

"Dennis, as you know the budget is going to be real tight this year and there will likely be more layoffs," he began. "Would you be willing to relocate if the right job came along?"

I knew what this meant, the end of my career at the INL.

"Of course Juan, I would enjoy a new challenge," I replied.

"Great, I'll be talking to managers at other Battelle sites and see what I can make happen," he said. I was encouraged about the prospect of a new job, but skeptical that Juan would pursue a job for me.

That evening I shared my concerns with LaVonna. She was hopeful. She commented, "You know, if someone at Juan's level wants it to happen, it will happen." Over the next several weeks we often talked about the possibility of living in a different city.

In late October, I met with Juan as a follow-up to our August meeting. From the outset of the meeting, I sensed a different tone than our previous discussion. Juan again noted the INL budget problems and its potential impact on the workforce.

"All of the Battelle operations are facing similar budget challenges," he emphasized.

I didn't say much. Towards the end of the meeting, Juan added, "At our next meeting we need to revisit the issue of your professional development and your future."

"OK, I will come prepared with some ideas and proposals," I said.

Chapter 72 – Michelle

In early August LaVonna, Dave Snell and I drove to Jackson Hole, Wyoming to see Michelle Obama speak at a fundraising event. By arriving a couple hours early we were able to stand within 20 feet of where she was speaking.

Michelle's speech was uplifting, and inspiring, especially when she spoke about the importance of educating our youth and our responsibility as parents. After her talk, she walked along the rope line and began shaking hands. The first hand she shook was Dave's. He was so surprised that he couldn't think of anything to say.

A few minutes later she clasped LaVonna's hand and smiled. LaVonna beamed as her eyes met Michelle's.

"Tell the President thank you for all he is doing for our country," she said. I was next to shake Michelle's hand. "God Bless and thank you," I said. The opportunity to speak to the First Lady was an experience that LaVonna and I will never forget. For me, it brought back memories of having shook the hand of Michelle's husband, aka President Obama, back in 2008. Perhaps one day we would get to meet Malia and Sasha.

Chapter 73 – Plutonium

In August, a friend of mine asked me to have breakfast with one of the employees involved in the November 8, 2011 plutonium event, Ralph Stanton. The three of us met at Bubba's barbeque restaurant. Ralph stood up to greet me. He was a big man with a big smile. As we sat down, his demeanor turned grim, "Dennis, I'm one of the two employees that got plutonium inside our bodies I'm the one that cut through the plastic, I was right there and breathed it in. This should have never happened. We did everything management told us to do. When the plutonium fell out and the alarms blared, we got out of there." Ralph spoke of the fear and anxiety that only comes when faced with one's own mortality.

Ralph said that he and the others were transported to the INL medical facility where the staff seemed incapable of explaining the danger of plutonium or the consequences of taking a so called therapy treatment called "chelation."

"You know Dennis, one of the things that makes me the maddest is that management knew prior to the job, that the hazard level had recently been increased from 'extremely unlikely' to "anticipated. If we knew this we would have never proceeded with the work as directed by management. Plus, we've learned that management was warned at least twice about the dangers of working with plutonium fuel plates and did nothing. I don't trust BEA when it says there will be no long term health effects,"

"BEA should have never allowed me and others to go home without being showered. Dennis, I've had samples of carpet, bedding and furniture from my home analyzed by an outside company. They found evidence of nuclear materials including plutonium 239 and americium 241. My wife and daughter have been breathing this stuff."

Ralph noted that his and other employee's initial bioassay samples from November 2011 were mishandled. He said he wouldn't trust BEA to do any further samples or analysis.

Sitting across the table from Ralph reminded me of the 1983 movie "Silkwood" starring Meryl Streep. Streep played the real life Karen Silkwood who worked making plutonium fuel rods for nuclear reactors. When Karen was exposed to radiation she conducted her own investigation and contacted the New York Times. Shortly thereafter, she died in a car accident on her way to meet with the reporter.

Ralph continued, "Dennis, I'm being harassed at work and threatened with disciplinary action because I'm speaking out about safety and health concerns. What should I do?"

"Ralph, there are protections for whistleblowers, but if you file a complaint BEA may come after you."

"I'm not afraid, I just want to know what helped you make it through.

"Ralph, what sustained me was my faith, family and friends."

In January 2012, the DOE Office of Health, Safety and Security issued the Accident Investigation. The following findings were included in the report, some of which validated information provided by Ralph.

- "The Board concluded that BEA failed to recognize the significance of and take appropriate action in response to available information regarding the material condition of the plutonium fuel plates."
- "The Board concluded that BEA does not have a process in place to promptly assess intakes of radioactive material for use in internal dose assessments and medical response to radiological emergencies."
- "The Board concluded that BEA does not have an effective program, for training cognizant personnel on certain radiological response activities (e.g., showering before special lung counts,

nose blowing) and communicating
radiological information (e.g. information
concerning bioassay samples.)"

- "The Board concluded that the DOE-ID
and BEA oversight systems were not
managed in such a way that they could
readily identify and correct legacy
deficiencies in the technical bases
supporting the ZPPR safety basis."

- The report also included the following:
"An offsite laboratory under contract
provided support in analyzing the
bioassay results. Site personnel stated
that due to miscommunication with the
offsite laboratory, the first samples sent
were not properly handled."

Chapter 74 – More Headlines

On October 5, 2012, the Post Register front page
headline was, "BEA is fined." The article continued,
"BEA was fined $412,500 for violations of quality
assurance requirements and occupational radiation
protection by DOE. The fine, which stemmed from two
2011 incidents involving worker radiation exposure was
announced Thursday. It was included in a letter from
John S. Boulder III, director of the DOE's Office of
Enforcement and Oversight to lab Director John
Grossenbacher. The letter said the exposure incidents
were of high safety significance."

"The incidents for which Battelle was fined
happened: On August 30, 2011 when an operator received

an elevated radiation dose to his right hand while processing fuel samples at the Materials and Fuels Complex's Hot Fuel Examination Facility – On November 8, 2011, when 16 workers were exposed to plutonium radiation at the building that once housed the Zero Power Physics Reactor at the MFC. At least one worker inhaled the radioactive substance."

Reading further the article stated, "INL officials said none of the 16 workers exposed in the November incident would experience adverse health problems as a result of the radiation exposure. They said the workers exposed to plutonium-239 in November had received radiation that was well within the DOE's annual regulatory limit."

(by Alex Stuckey).

This was the first time that the public was made aware of the August 30, 2011 incident. Perhaps it was because BEA senior management didn't think it was a big deal for an employee to be exposed to "elevated radiation."

On October 12, 2012 the front page headline was, "Fines to Battelle total 1.17 mil." The article continued, "The DOE has fined BEA a total of 1.17 million for violations of security and Nuclear Safety regulations assessed during the past 19 months. Of the 15 contractors evaluated by DOE's Office of Enforcement Battelle's work at INL is the only one that has received four fines for remittance over that time frame."

"Upon reviewing Office of Enforcement violation and consent orders the Post Register discovered a $425,000 fine issued to Battelle in 2011. The fine stemmed from a 2009 security violation and was not previously disclosed or reported publically. Alvarez said the sanction

likely did not bring much attention because the incident
was not perceived to be a big deal...The final notice of
violation from the DOE stated that classified information
was compromised, which led to unauthorized access to the
information. Battelle department and project managers
failed to adhere to the classification officer's repeated
warnings about the project, the notice said. The notice
also stated that Battelle's personnel placed more emphasis
on meeting the customer's demands than performing
classified work securely. "It was only one instance' (of
security violations) Alvarez said. We've had none since
then. " (Reporter, Alex Stuckey)

This security violation caused great consternation
in the work place. How could a senior manager, say that
mishandling classified information wasn't a big deal. In
the opinion of many, this was just a sad excuse for not
informing the employees or the public. The fact remained
that BEA was fined $425,000 and BEA thought it wasn't
important enough to let anyone know. Equally troubling,
was the fact that management ignored the warnings of the
classification officer, apparently because it was more
important to meet scheduled milestones. Of course,
meeting milestones leads to better award fees and higher
bonuses for senior management.

All of this bad news was coming to light at the
same time that the Department of Energy was in the midst
of deciding whether or not to extend the contract to have
BEA manage the laboratory for another five years. The
decision was already past due and throughout the INL
employees were speculating was to what DOE would do.
Many believed that DOE would extend the contract but
was simply waiting for things to die down before making
the announcement. I was one of the employees who

believed this.

Chapter 75 – My Career II

For my scheduled November meeting with Juan, I came prepared with a one page "white paper" which included my employment history, experience and education. I also identified specific INL jobs that I was qualified for and interested in. For the first time, I included the Employee Concerns Program Manager and Ethics Officer positions. Until now, I had never explicitly stated an interest in these jobs because I believed that BEA would never consider me. However, at this point I had nothing to lose. I also included in the white paper the possibility of being the manager of the diversity and/or employee relations (ER) organization. I handed the paper to Juan at the beginning of our meeting. He glanced at it, but left it on the table and began writing on his whiteboard. This gave me the impression that his mind was already made up.

"Dennis, you don't have the breadth and depth of experience to manage an ER function, and diversity is no longer a focus area for Battelle," Juan said.

"So, what about going back to do what I used to do,' I asked.

"I don't think that would work," he responded. Juan was careful not to mention why it wouldn't work.

For most of the meeting, I was trying to absorb what all of this meant. I concluded that Juan was preparing the groundwork for laying me off. I wondered if this would be our last meeting.

The week before Christmas, during a management

workshop, I visited with John Peterson. John was hired as the Employee Concerns Program manager in March 2009, just two days before the DOE appeal decision. More recently, he had been transferred to supervisor of audits. I asked John if he missed being the ECP manager. "Sometimes,' he responded. For no apparent reason, he mentioned his first days at the INL. As he had told me once before, on his second day of employment he picked up the newspaper and read that I had won the appeal of my whistleblower complaint.

"To this day, I am still angry that no one told me about the pending complaint prior to being hired," he said. "Had I known, I would have never accepted the job."

It had been almost four years since John was hired as the ECP manager and he still remembered this event like it was yesterday. He also noted that when he was hired he had no experienced with employee concerns work. John's words haunted me for the next few days. The pain of years past resurfaced as memories flooded my thoughts. I lay awake at night praying for peace of mind and a forgiving spirit.

I was looking forward to the week off between Christmas and New Years. The stress of the impending layoff and the conversations with Juan made for long days at work. On December 20, 2012 management released an iNote. The note told us what we already knew. There would be a layoff in early 2013.

Chapter 76 – "2012 MLK Banquet, "I Challenge You, Idaho Falls"

This year we were fortunate to have as our keynote speaker, Dr. Freeman Hrabowksi III, President, University Maryland Baltimore County. TIME magazine had named Hrabowski "One of the 100 most influential people in the world" in 2012. At the age of twelve, Freeman had been arrested and jailed for twelve days for participating in a children's civil rights march with Dr. King.

The morning of the banquet, Freeman had breakfast with the African American Alliance at the Wasabi Grill. He encouraged the young people in attendance to consider majoring in math, science and engineering. At the end of the breakfast, he gave Jasmine and another young lady a math problem and challenged them to have the correct answer by the time of the banquet. To his delight, both gave him the right answer just prior to his keynote address.

The audience was enthralled with Dr. Hrabowski's keynote address. He began with, "My message is very simple. The way we think about ourselves as a country, as a community, here in Idaho Falls, as individuals and families, the way we talk about ourselves, the language that we use, the values that we hold will be so important. We become those things, they determine our destiny."

Freeman spoke about the importance of math, science and engineering, especially for our children. He said, "The challenge is to help children of all races get that education. If they get the education, all things are possible.

He commented about Idaho Falls, "This is a community where people care about each other. Here is a community where you have a Dr. King celebration and you have all races here, because they believe in it and believe in themselves."

His closed with the following, "I challenge you Idaho Falls, to watch your thoughts, they become your words, watch your words because they become your actions, watch your actions because they become your habits, and watch your habits because they become your character. Character becomes destiny, dreams and values. Idaho Falls, you are a very special community and you can become even better."

Chapter 77 – A Bad Beginning

On February 11, 2013, several friends stopped by my cubicle. They informed me that there was an incident in one of the buildings in town. During an experiment at least one employee was severely burned and had been taken to the hospital. The chemical that caused the burn was believed to be some type of molten salt. Employees wondered whether BEA would inform the public, and if so, when.

Around this same time, a friend told me about an

event at the Advanced Test Reactor. He told me that an employee had recently been terminated and escorted from the premises. Allegedly, this employee had stated that he had (or could) sabotaged some computer code in the training module of the reactor. Supposedly, someone overheard him say that if he were to be laid off the code was set to cause problems in the reactor. If he were not laid off, he would reset the code such that no problems would occur. According to rumor, the FBI was conducting an investigation of this event.

I never found out if the alleged sabotage was true, but within a couple days the subject employee was no longer an INL employee.

I spent the next week cleaning up my desk and work files. I prepared for what I believed was my eminent departure from the INL. I brought home a couple of boxes of personal effects, including pictures, awards and certificates of appreciation accumulated over the past 32 years. As I walked the halls, I wondered what life would be like without a job at the INL.

Chapter 78 – Full Circle

On Sunday, February 13, LaVonna and I attended church as usual.

At the close of his sermon, Pastor Bob informed us that there were several members of a family that would be baptized. He asked the family to gather around the baptismal pool at the front of the sanctuary. To my surprise and delight Loren and his wife went forward.

Bob baptized five of their children. At the conclusion of the baptism Bob invited friends to congratulate the family. LaVonna and I went forward and gave Loren and his wife a hug and wished God's blessings upon them.

In my heart, I knew that this was meant to be part of my story. It wasn't just by chance or happenstance that Loren had called the BEA hotline, almost exactly eight years ago. Loren had been placed in my path for a reason. I was a better person for having gone through the experience.

Chapter 79 – The Last Mile

The week of March 4th I spent time doing a goodbye tour. I stopped by the offices of friends and colleagues. I told them I would be laid off within the next few days. It was difficult saying good bye. For all its challenges, the INL is a place filled with great people doing great work. I would miss being part of the INL family.

Tuesday morning March 12, I awoke shortly before 7:00 a.m. and prepared for work. I checked my iPhone. Exactly at 7:00 a.m. an iNote was delivered to all employees, "Involuntary Separations will begin today." I woke up LaVonna, "Sweetheart, today is the day."

Before leaving, LaVonna and I prayed together. "I love you, God will be with you," she said.

I arrived at my desk at 8:00 a.m. At 8:10 a.m. my phone rang. "Juan needs to meet with you right away," Kelli, Juan's assistant, said. I called LaVonna, "I just got the call, I'll be home soon."

I entered Juan's office, the tension was palpable. I could hear Juan's labored breathing as he prepared to speak. I took a seat at the round table. Juan took a seat on the other side, a little further away than usual. We had sat at this table many times over the past three years.

This was nothing like those meetings. Juan's voice was strained as he began the obviously well-rehearsed script. It took less than 60 seconds.

"As part of a skill set realignment required to perform our mission efficiently within the levels funding provided by various customers, there is a need to reduce INL's workforce through an Involuntary Separation process. Your position is impacted by this reduction and is being eliminated," he said.

"Can I or Kelli help you with packing or taking stuff to your car?"

"No thanks, I already took everything home except for my family picture," I told him. Juan was surprised that I knew I was being laid off and that I had taken all necessary actions.

"Is there anything I can do?" Juan asked.

"No thanks, it is finished," I replied. We shook hands and I left his office.

I returned to my cubicle to get my personal affects and to say goodbye to friends and colleagues. The first thing I did was retrieve two draft emails I had prepared. The first was addressed to approximately two hundred employees, "Well, it's been a long journey here at the laboratory. I feel blessed to have been part of this great institution and even more blessed to have known each of

you. Today is my last day as an INL employee. While a
bit sad, I leave knowing that God will continue to lead my
life and bless me with new challenges and opportunities. I
wish and pray the best for the laboratory. Always
remember: Faith, Family, Friends."

A good friend, Sammy Tawfik, responded, "Your
kindness and life example were light for so many around
the Lab. I will miss you around here. But, I hope to see
you when you can and learn from you how God continues
to use you. Best wishes to you."

The second email I addressed to approximately 15
colleagues. As a group, with the support of senior
management, we had developed a set of "INL Values."

These values would provide the foundation for
improved decision making and help build trust in the work
place and the community. The four values were: Integrity,
Excellence, Teamwork, and Ownership. The values had
been reviewed by Grossenbacher, and were ready to be
communicated to employees.

The roll out of the values was scheduled for April.
Grossenbacher would personally endorse the values and
express BEA's commitment to the highest standards of
ethical conduct.

Herein was the problem. In the opinion of many,
including myself, Grossenbacher was no longer the
appropriate spokesperson for the values. During the past
couple of weeks a rumor was rampant throughout the
laboratory. The rumor was that Grossenbacher had failed
to live up to the standards that he himself had established.

Employees remembered Grossenbacher's October

5, 2010 iNote, when he terminated senior manager, Dwayne Coburn, "This action is a result of failure to achieve leadership and standards that are an expectation of leaders and managers at INL."

My concern was not with the truthfulness of the rumor, my concern was that most employees seemed to believe it was true. In my opinion, and that of many other employees, Grossenbacher' endorsement of the values would risk ridicule. In my email, I suggested that BEA find another way to communicate the values. This email was my last official act as an INL employee.

A Security staff member escorted me from the second floor of the building to the front entrance. I felt like John Coffey from the movie "The Green Mile" as he walked his final walk, to the electric chair.

The two mile drive home seemed to be in slow motion. As I turned into the neighborhood I thought, "I'm almost there." I wanted, no, I needed to be home. When I entered the door, Lavonna was there waiting for me. We embraced tightly as tears streamed down our faces.

Quotes from Notable Persons in the Book

John Denson, President of Lockheed Martin Idaho Technologies

"I wanted someone that would dig their heels in and do that job right, because it's the way Lockheed Martin operates. They want ethical conduct out of everybody. And since, the President's responsible for everything, well, I had to have somebody I thought was of high character

and good moral standing and ethical background. He
satisfied all those things for me."

Dr. Jim Lake, former BEA Director, Nuclear Science and Technology, former President of American Nuclear Society.

"Thanks Dennis, you've been wonderful to work with, and
you've made it easy for us managers to do the right thing."

Dr. Pete Miller, DOE Assistant Secretary Nuclear Energy

"Dennis Patterson has become a new friend and so has his
lovely wife."

Sheila Olsen, Idaho Commission on Human Rights, Interfaith Community Service Project

"Congratulations Dennis! What a wonderful example of
faith, courage, perseverance, patience, and standing for
right this is! I am so happy for you and so proud to call
you my friend."

Epilogue

INL/DOE

Early in my journey I knew that I would one day write a book. Being involuntarily terminated from the INL gave me the freedom to do so. I wrote this book for the same reason I filed the whistleblower complaint. My hope is that shedding light on the ills of the Idaho National Laboratory will lead to a better laboratory. I hope that the laboratory will learn to treat employees with respect and that it will operate with integrity and transparency. I hope the Department of Energy will recognize that the whistleblower process is broken and currently serves the interest of the contractors rather than the employees and the nation. Americans have a right to know what is happening at DOE facilities that are funded by their tax dollars.

Since my last day at the INL I have continued to do what I can to help others as they fight instances of injustice and unfair treatment. Over the past year I have been contacted by several former BEA employees for advice and assistance. Each of them had been recently terminated. All of them believed that their dismissal was either unjust and/or retaliation for reporting misconduct. Several of them were referred to me by the DOE-Idaho Employee Concerns Manager.

Two of the terminated employees filed formal whistleblower complaints. One was dismissed by DOE and the other resulted in a formal hearing that was held here in Idaho Falls. My good friend and fellow whistleblower Ralph Stanton agreed to be a witness for the plaintiff, Alison Marschman. A few days after BEA learned that he was going to testify, he was terminated from his job, two days before Christmas.

On the morning of January 8, 2014 Ralph called me and asked if I would be willing to be present during his testimony. It was a privilege to be asked to attend for a couple reasons. First, Ralph was a person of conviction and integrity. Second, I had advised Alison about her case and believed that she too was a person of great character. Prior to being terminated in 2013 she worked as a Health Physics Technician protecting the safety and health of her fellow BEA employees.

When I entered the courtroom I took a seat in the back. Seated at the front of the room to my right was BEA attorney, Adam Andersen, and Larry Halverson. Yes, the same Larry Halverson that had represented BEA in my whistleblower case. The Hearing Officer immediately stopped the proceedings and asked who had just entered the room. When I responded, "Dennis Patterson," I was told that the hearing was closed to the public and that I needed to leave. Although I believed the Hearing Officer was wrong to kick me out I apologized and exited the courtroom.

Later that afternoon I placed a call to the Director of the DOE Office of Hearing and Appeals, Poli Marmolejos. I left a voice mail explaining my concern and asked for a return phone call. On Friday, January 10, Marmlejos called me. He apologized for my being asked to leave the hearing. He noted that DOE is committed to transparency and that in most all cases the public is able to attend whistleblower cases. He went on to say that Hearing Officers have the discretion to close the proceedings if they deem it appropriate. He didn't express an opinion as to whether it was appropriate for this particular hearing to be closed, but he assured me he would follow up on the matter. One thing I knew for certain is that the media did not report on the hearing. Most likely because neither DOE nor BEA informed them.

In another matter the Post Register ran a headline on December 12, 2013, "EX-INL worker awarded $100,000." The jury found that the employee's "perceived mental disability" was a motivating factor for BEA to take adverse employment actions against him. The article noted that according to court records, management had allegedly asked the employee to "engage in behavior that he deemed unethical and inappropriate." The employee was a nuclear engineer. He resigned in October 2011, "because of the hostile work environment and discrimination at INL." I later learned that the plaintiff's attorney was my friend and former attorney, DeAnne Casperson. Once again, she had prevailed in proving that a BEA employee had been treated unfairly.

In February 2014 I was an invited speaker at the National Association of Employee Concerns Professionals (NAECP) Winter Conference in San Francisco. Before being involuntarily removed as the Ethics Employee Concerns manager for the INL I was a member. It was an honor to share my experience as a whistleblower with an organization that is committed to creating a safe work culture within Nuclear Utilities, the Department of Energy and the Petroleum industry.

On March 28 DOE announced that it had extended BEA's contract to operate and manage the INL.

The DOE said the decision was based on BEA's "proven performance and success" in managing the site. Members of Idaho's Congressional Delegation issued a press release, "BEA's Extension at INL Well-Deserved." Most of the employees I spoke to were very disheartened and disappointed, but no one seem surprised. Folks had come to expect the worst and this was it.

The Power of Hope

The first part of 2014 was special time for myself and many others in the Idaho Falls community. The theme for the Dr. King banquet was "The Power of Hope." The keynote speaker was our own Dr. Lucretia Murphy. Lucretia arrived with her parents in Idaho Falls when she was a young child in the early 1970's. She excelled scholastically and was Idaho's 1988 Junior Miss, and third runner up in America's Junior Miss competition. Lucretia went on to earn a law degree and a Ph.D in higher education policy.

Dr. Murphy's passion and career pursuit was to educate America's youth, particularly those most in need of help or a second chance. Lucretia served as the Executive Director of the See Forever Foundation and Maya Angelou Public Charter School in Washington D.C. She had also served as Program Director for Youth Transitions for Jobs for the Future in Boston, MA. Lucretia continues her work with youth and adults as a Program Director with Jobs for the Future's Building Economic Opportunity Group. She now lives in Tampa, Florida.

The banquet room was filled to capacity. Lucretia opened her talk by giving honor to her parents, "my mom was the best teacher at Idaho Falls High School." She noted that her father was a chemist at the Idaho National Laboratory and one time president of the local NAACP. Giving tribute to Dr. King she said, "I believe and affirm that Martin Luther King was an American hero, who helped the nation realize its better ideals and helped all of us realize our better selves." Dr. Murphy encouraged all of us to "remember who you are and where you came from." A statement she made still rings in my ears, "the power of hope helps people in the pit of darkness keep going." At the close of her talk the audience gave her a standing ovation.

As usual, some of the proceeds from the banquet were used to award scholarships to graduating young people furthering their educational pursuits. I met three of the recipients at the annual awards breakfast. I was so inspired that I wanted to share just a brief part of their individual stories.

Ibukun Omotowa: "We came to the United States, specifically Moscow, Idaho when I was only 1 years old. My earliest memories come from a time when my family needed government assistance. The realities of our house being vandalized, of our bikes being stolen, and of being harassed because of our ethnicity. As I grew up and became aware of these things, I began to take note of who I am in this big tapestry of America. Growing up as a Nigerian and as a Black American in the largely Caucasian state of Idaho for almost all of my life has sculpted my personal life in a colossal fashion. I've been blessed with the opportunity to live at a cultural crossroads, to see the best and the worst of all walks of life. I must never let this blessing go to waste." Ibukun will be attending Harvard University majoring in biomedical engineering.

Kai Amos: "Idaho Falls is a community where in
order to succeed everyone has to follow the same path;
however, I have taken my conservative community and
used it to my advantage in becoming the woman I am
today. I take all my experiences – positive and negative –
and turn them into constructive building blocks for me to
be the best person I can be. My aspiration is to be a
positive influence on others. I have learned how to
positively influence others by taking a stand, using my
voice, and teaching. I will make a difference." Kai will
attend Washington State University to become a Doctor of
Veterinary Medicine.

Charlyn Hess: "For my senior project I worked
with special needs students and helped them experience
real life situations. It was a very rewarding experience. I
plan to work with people with disabilities and help them
understand who they are what they are going through."
Charlyn's story is even more remarkable because when she
was born she wasn't expected to live and then was never
expected to walk. She lived, walked, and is now pursuing a
certification as a medical assistant at Eastern Idaho
Technical College.

Conclusion

It is my hope that the stories and people in this
book inspires others to be their best and do their best, not
just for themselves but for others as well. I believe I did
the right things for the right reasons. I have told my story
and can now feel at peace. As Maya Angelou famously
said, "There is no greater agony that bearing an untold

story inside of you."

ABOUT THE AUTHOR

Dennis Patterson, was born and raised in Idaho Falls, Idaho, home of the Department of Energy's Idaho National Laboratory (INL). He began his career as a laborer at the INL in the early seventies when he was still in high school. He continued working as a laborer during summers while attending Idaho State University where he graduated with a degree in business management. After graduating he worked at the laboratory for the next thirty two years. For thirteen years he served as the "Ethics Officer" and Employee Concerns manager. He is a member of the Ethics and Compliance Officer Association, an organization dedicated to the principles of Integrity, Confidentiality, Collegiality and Cooperation. He is also a member of the National Association of Employee Concerns Professionals, an organization committed to creating a safety work culture within the Department of Energy and other high risk industries.

Dennis's experience as a whistleblower at the INL compelled him to write this book such that others could learn and benefit from his story and perhaps create a better and safer work environment at Department of Energy laboratories across the nation.